Reflections on Surah

AL 'IMRAN

A Thematic Understanding

ANIS AHMAD

E ISLAMIC FOUNDATION

Reflections on Surah Al 'Imran: A Thematic Understanding

First published in England by
The Islamic Foundation
Markfield Conference Centre
Ratby Lane, Markfield
Leicestershire, LE67 9SY United Kingdom

Tel: +44 (0) 1530 249230

Quran House, PO Box 30611, Kenya

P.M.B 3193 Kano, Nigeria

Website: www.kubepublishing.com
Email: info@kubepublishing.com

Cataloguing-in-Publication Data is available from the British Library

ISBN Paperback 978-0-86037-993-5
ISBN Ebook 978-0-86037-998-0

Cover Design and Typesetting: Nasir Cadir
Stock Image: Istock

Contents

- » Acknowledgements v
- » Preface vii
- » The Context 1
- » An Overview 3
- » *Tawhid*: The Common Theme in All Divine Scriptures 5
- » The Qur'an as a Touchstone for Truth 9
- » The Wisdom Behind *Naskh*, Qualification of *Ayat* 11
- » Avoiding an Immoderate, Lavish and Prodigal Living 15
- » Success of Truth Over Falsehood 16
- » Invitation to Use Reason (*Ta'aqul*), Critical Thinking, Contemplation (*Tafakkur*) and Introspection (*Tadabbur*) 20
- » Realization of *Tawhid* as a Matter of Faith, and a Way of Life 22
- » Unity and Variety 24
- » The Culture of Freedom of Faith and Unity in Variety 25
- » Bani Isra'il's Delusions 29
- » The Ethics of Intercommunal Relations 30
- » Interfaith Relationship 31
- » No Intercession 35
- » Kind and Hospitable Attitude Towards Unbelievers 36
- » Holding of Key Positions 37
- » Obedience to the Prophet ﷺ 38

» Prophet Isa's Clear Message 45
» The Qur'anic Invitation for a Dialogue 48
» Invitation to Return to the Original Faith 51
» The Original Faith of Mankind 55
» The Path of Ibrahim 59
» Three Commonalities 61
» The First House of Worship 62
» The Behavioural Outcome of Attachment to Allah Through Hajj 64
» Dimensions of the Word *Ayah* 64
» The Leadership Role of the Muslims 68
» Faith, Unity and Ethical Role of the Muslims 69
» Some Implications of *Khayra Ummah* 73
» Muslims as a Qualitative Community 76
» Outcomes of *Da'wah* 78
» The Culture of *Ma'ruf* and Elimination of Social Evils 81
» Universal Principles of Good Governance and Organizational Excellence 88
» The Negative Role of the *Munafiqun* 90
» The Dynamic Role of the Prophet ﷺ 91
» Elevation of the Martyrs (*Shuhada'*) 93
» The Attitude of *Munafiqun* 95
» The Supplication 100
» Take-home Points 103

Acknowledgements

The credit for this work goes to an unknown teacher who wrote a letter outlining her wish for me to write a simple elaboration of the Quranic message for the youth. For over thirty years, my commitments with the institutions of higher learning in their academic matters could not allow me time to devote to this noble task. I thank Allah for allowing me to at least make a beginning in this direction. It is up to Him to permit the project to reach its completion.

I appreciate the encouragement I received from my wife, Anisa, and my children while working on the project for long hours away from them in my library. I also recognise the help I received from Huzefa Khalid, my staff, in typing and retyping the manuscript. I am also thankful to Saarah Ismail, for copy editing, and Haris, for his personal interest in the publication of this and other volumes. I also appreciate the assistance I received in review of the manuscript by Mr Arshad Ahmad Baig and Dr Hafiz Sohaib Zafar Malik.

May Allah reward all of them for their help, patience and contribution.

I dedicate this volume to my spiritual mentors, Sayyed Abul 'Ala Mawdudi and Amin Ahsan Islahi.

Wama taufiqi illa bi Allah.

Prof. Anis Ahmad Ph D
March 23, 2025

Preface

We are living in an age of individualism. From early childhood, a person goes through an indoctrination in an invisible manner, in the name of personal liberty and freedom. The early training of mind and manners manifests itself in an entrepreneurial behaviour of maximising for oneself wealth, comfort, enjoyment, and glamour. Not much importance is given to the inculcation of a sense of social accountability, sacrifice, respect for the wellbeing of others, helping out the needy, the poor, the orphans and the elderly and less privileged. Everyone is supposed to work for her/himself. Even in married life, a husband and wife remain as individuals; as I and you, and not as we.

Some of the world religions also follow an approach of individual redemption, salvation and enlightenment. Everyone is supposed to be his/her own Buddha. Islam creates a balance and moderation between the individual, family, society and state. The individual is considered in the context of family; as a son or daughter, father or mother, brother or sister, uncle or aunt, grandfather or grandmother and so on. Family is not nuclear but extended. The individual is ethically and legally responsible for the welfare of the family. Family plays a foundational role in the transfer of values, culture, and social obligations. At the same time, every believer, male or female, is made responsible for social welfare and the wellbeing of all members of society.

The Qur'an as the guidance (*hidayah*) for mankind looks on human beings holistically and prescribes an ethical code of conduct for all human beings. It defines the purpose and objective of human life on Earth in terms of global ethical principles of unity (*tawhid*) in life, realization of equity and fairness (*'adl*), respect and promotion of life (*nafs*), observance of rational behaviour (*'aql*), freedom to choose and practice a way of life (*din*), respect of human genealogy (*nasl, nasab*) and protection of property (*mal*).

The Qur'an provides ethical and legal guidelines for these seven objectives of humanity irrespective of colour, race, geographic region, sex, ethnicity, marital status or faith of an individual and society. The revelations (*wahi-al-Qur'an*) received by the Prophet ﷺ in Madinah, particularly addresses social, economic, political, cultural, legal and environmental issues faced by humanity. The Qur'an is not a book which focuses on some indigenous issues, it is a universal guidance having direct relevance with social, economic, political, legal and cultural issues faced by human beings at a global level.

Surah al-Baqarah, surah Al 'Imran, al-Nisa and al-Mai'dah encompass a significant part of the socio economic, legal and political issues faced by mankind. This brief volume consisting of *surah Al 'Imran* provides valuable guidance on problems and issues faced by a growing Muslim community in a multi-religious, pluralistic context.

The guidance provided in the *surah* is not particular to the early developing Muslim society in Madinah. It has direct relevance with human behaviour and conduct in a techno-cultural society. Its principles and guidance transcend space and time.

This thematic study of the third *surah* in sequence is an attempt to contextualize the *surah* and discover its inner connectivity and cohesion.

The Context

This *surah* was revealed in Madinah when the Muslim community (*ummah*) was still in its formative period. The victory in the Battle of Badr (2 AH) conveyed a clear message to the Makkans and others, including the surrounding Jewish tribes, that Islam was no more a faith belonging to an emigrant group (*Muhajirun*) and their helpers (*Ansar*) who were the residents of what was earlier known as Yathrib (and now called *Madinat al-Nabi* or the town of the Prophet ﷺ, commonly referred to as *al-Madinah*), but one that was a thriving community with a living force, a universal message and an ideology. The believers were not an inward-looking faith group but a forward-looking dynamic *ummah* with a mission:

"*You are now the best people brought forth for [the guidance and leadership of] mankind and you enjoin what is right and forbid what is wrong and believe in Allah.*" (Al 'Imran 3: 110)

They were given the huge responsibility of changing the direction of history and of establishing an ethical and moral order founded on the Divine guidance of the Qur'an and upon the model behaviour and conduct of Allah's final Messenger ﷺ.

In *Surah al-Baqarah*, the symbolic change of direction of the *qiblah*—from Quds to the centre of Abrahamic *da'wah,* Makkah—was announced, which was actually an indication of the transfer of leadership of mankind from the Bani Isra'il to the Muslim *ummah*. The tribes of Bani Isra'il surrounding Madinah could not easily reconcile with or adjust to this new reality. The Makkans' defeat in Badr followed by dislocation of the Jewish neighbouring tribe of Banu Qaynuqa, due to their defiance of the covenant of Madinah, strengthened feelings of retribution and revenge in the Makkans as well as in the Jewish neighbours. Added to this were the hypocrites (*munafiqun*) who pretended to be Muslims but in reality, were enemies of Islam. The chief of Banu Nadir, Ka'ab ibn al-Ashraf, disregarded the age-old alliance with the people of Yathrib and blatantly violated the covenant of Madinah, and continuously conspired with the Makkans.

It was to this backdrop, in the third year of the Hijrah, that the Battle of Uhud took place and on which *Surah Al 'Imran* makes a critical review. The *surah*, like *Surah al-Baqarah*, begins with the core message of *tawhid*. To a great extent, it carries forward the basic themes of *al-Baqarah*. Both *surahs* begin with the syllables '*Alif Lam Mim*' and a statement of the Divine origin of the Qur'an, the supremacy of Allah, and the leadership role of the Muslim *ummah*. *Al-Baqarah* refers extensively to the history of the rise and fall of the Bani Isra'il, while *Al 'Imran* focuses more on the deviance of Christians from their own scripture. The *surah* invites the People of the Book (both the Jews and the Christians) to a dialogue based on the two common foundations of Abrahamic faith i.e., belief in the absolute unity of Allah, the Creator of mankind and the universe; and the inevitability of the final ethical judgement in the Hereafter (*Akhirah*).

An Overview

Surah Al 'Imran, in sequence, is the third *surah* in the Qur'an. It was revealed in Madinah during a critical period. Consisting of 200 verses (*ayat*), it was revealed in segments, like other *surahs*. The first group of *ayat* was revealed after the Battle of Badr (2 AH/624 CE), while the last segment of *ayat* came after the Battle of Uhud (3 AH/625 CE). The section dealing with the family of 'Imran, addressing the Christians was most probably revealed in 9 AH/630 CE when a delegation of Christians from Najran, Yemen visited Madinah.

The *surah* was revealed in a tumultuous period and addresses issues that relate to the consolidation of faith (*iman*). A critical review is made of the performance of the Companions (*Sahabah*) in the Battle of Uhud. The leadership role of the Muslim community and the importance of commanding good (*da'wah*, *amr bi al-ma'ruf*) and forbidding evil (*nahi 'an al-munkar*) is emphasized. A dialogue with the Bani Isra'il is initiated and mention is made of the elevated station of the family of 'Imran. Additionally, the importance of consultation (*shura*) in governance is elaborated.

The *surah*, like *al-Baqarah*, begins with a statement of basic Islamic faith in Allah the Ever-Living, the Self-Sustaining. Who alone sustains the whole of the universe; Who, earlier, revealed the Torah and the Evangels for the guidance of mankind. It focuses on the attributes of Allah namely, Ever-Living and Self-Sustaining, and indicates that no other than Allah enjoys these two attributes.

The *surah* offers a critical review of the *Sahabah*'s performance in Uhud. When studied in the light of the Battle of Badr, it offers guidelines to not only the *Sahabah* but to all the believers in situations of crisis.

The success of the Muslims in the Battle of Badr was no less than a miracle. The strength of the *Sahabah* was hardly one-third when compared to the Makkan invaders, and the former were least equipped with weapons. Yet they were able to defeat a highly equipped force of Makkans three times their number. This was possible only with special support from Allah. In the critical situation of Uhud, when 'Abdullah ibn Ubayy suddenly withdrew along with his 300 followers, and only 700 believers were left to face a well-equipped army of 3,000 warriors, the *Sahabah* were confident that with Allah's help, they would overcome the Makkans. The Messenger ﷺ of Allah made his war plans and, in order to protect any attack of the Makkans from behind, placed fifty archers at the mountain pass.

With complete trust in Allah's help, the *Sahabah* encountered the enemy. The Makkans could not resist them despite their well-equipped army, and they started to retreat and disperse. This was interpreted by the *Sahabah* as their victory, and they began to collect the war spoils. The contingent of archers at the mountain pass also thought the war was over and started to make a move, even though their commander insisted that they should not leave the mountain pass, as directed by the Prophet ﷺ. Khalid ibn al-Walid, an experienced commander of the Makkan force, detected this weak point. He led his contingent of riders to go around the mountain and attack the Muslims from behind. This turned the Muslims' victory into a state of confusion, causing a heavy loss of life to the Muslim army. Abu Sufyan thought they had taken their revenge, therefore instructed the Makkan army to return to Makkah. The Prophet ﷺ, as a war strategist, commanded the horse riders to follow the Makkans in order to convey to them the message that the Muslims are not subdued and are strong to combat further with the Makkans. The *surah* offers a critical appraisal of the conflict which provides great lessons for the believers to learn from.

While *Surah al-Baqarah* refers frequently to the Bani Isra'il and reminds them of their violation of their covenant with their Lord, *Surah Al 'Imran* invites the Christians to the original message of 'Isa. In this respect, the *surah* refers to the original teachings of 'Isa who worshiped none but Allah and who denounced all false gods associated with Allah. It also refers to the miraculous births of 'Isa and Yahya [John the Baptist] and the elevation of Maryam above all women of the world.

The *surah* also offers a common ground for dialogue with the People of the Book, by taking the faith of Ibrahim as the basis, who followed the Straight Path (*din hanif*) and who associated none with Allah. The *surah* indicates that Islam is the continuation and culmination of the message of Ibrahim, Musa and 'Isa.

The *surah* addresses the Muslim community as '*khayrah ummah*', i.e., the best community created for the dissemination and realization of all that is ethically good (*ma'ruf*) and for the removal of all that is unethical and immoral (*munkar*). It wants believers to hold fast to the Qur'an and the Prophetic Sunnah in order to succeed in this world and in the life to come.

The *surah* also provides guidance on good governance through a system based on mutual consultation (*shura*).

Tawhid: The Common Theme in All Divine Scriptures

One major theme of the Qur'an is the universality of the *Shari'ah* or presence of certain basic themes in the teachings of the earlier Prophets. Most of the earlier commandments are revalidated by the Qur'an, as evidence of the unity in Truth. While highly critical of associationism (*shirk*) and dualism, Islam takes a forward-looking, positive approach of gradually moving from what may be common to what is different. It is an inclusive and not an exclusive approach. The *surah*, like *al-Baqarah*, also begins with these letters *alif*, *lam*, *mim*. As elaborated in reflections on *al-Baqarah*, use of these expressions was particular to Arabic literature of high literary quality. Obviously, Allah's *kalam* transcends all possible categories of literature. The real meaning of these letters used is known only to Allah. No known literary expert of pre-Islamic Arabic even questioned the meaning of these syllables.

Perhaps the message was that you who are proud of your Arabic literary excellence and know these letters, do your best to create from them speech like the Qur'an. And none of you can forge even an *ayah* similar to the

Qur'an. This is followed by a statement of fact which is a major key theme of the Qur'an namely *tawhid*, "*There is no deity except Allah, the Ever-Living [al-Hayy], the Eternal Master [al-Qayyum].*" (Al 'Imran 3: 2) These two personal attributes of Allah ﷻ mentioned at the outset in this *surah* are the basic themes of all later dialogues and deliberations between the followers of *tawhid* and others. The name *al-Hayy* refers to the One and Only who is Ever-Living and Ever-Present: "*All faces shall be humbled before the Ever-Living, Self-Sustaining Lord...*". (Ta Ha 20: 111) Here the attribute, the Everlasting Lord, is complemented with another Divine attribute that He is Self-Sustaining, or in other words, One who exists by Himself, who remains alive without any food and support and who is without any change. The Qur'an specifies: "*[O Prophet] put your trust in Him who is Ever-Living; He will never die and glorify Him with His Praise.*" (al-Furqan 25: 58) A similar message is conveyed at another place in the Qur'an: "*He is Ever-Living—there is no god but He—so call upon Him, consecrating to Him all your devotion. All praise and thanks be to Allah, Lord of all worlds.*" (Ghafir 40: 65) The two attributes of Allah mentioned here invite human intellect to ponder and use these two attributes as a measuring rod for accepting any being as God. Nothing in nature and the universe is ever-living or self-sustaining. Same is the case in the human world. No human being, pious or non-pious, remains in one state. We cannot think of a person who has no dependency for his/her existence. A person is either the son/daughter, father/mother, or brother/sister of another person. Consequently, no mortal who depends on others for their own identity can be totally independent and self-sustaining.

The emphasis on these two personal attributes of Allah, Ever-Living and Self-Sustaining, clearly indicates the inconsistency in the Jewish belief in God's imminence or manifestation in the human form of Prophet 'Uzayr [Ezra]; the same can be said about the Christian dogma of 'Isa [Jesus] as Lord, sharing in Divinity, yet crucified before he rose from his grave to share supper with the companions. The beauty of the Qur'an is in its terseness and its non-theological discourse which appeals to human reason and heart at the same time. If Ibrahim, Ishaq, Ya'qub, Musa and 'Isa, all declared that they believed in the Lord who is Ever-Living, Ever-Subsisting, then how could 'Uzayr [Ezra] who passed away and had parents be taken as God incarnate by the Jews? How can 'Isa, who was given birth by Maryam, be called Lord and son of God, when the Creator God simply means One who neither begets nor is begotten?

The word *hayat*, from the root letters *h-y-y*, means life. One of its different forms, *ahyahu*, meaning 'he gave life to him' indicates the presence of one who causes life and who alone is the source of all that exists. As an attribute of Allah, al-Hayy therefore refers to the One who gives life and controls it, and One who is always living, while no change can come to Him. In simple words, no mortal can be assigned this attribute.

Without going into details of the implications of the two attributes of the Creator, with which this *surah* begins, it maintains that this Book, the Qur'an is revealed and sent down to the Prophet ﷺ by none other than the Ever-Living and the Self-Subsisting Lord of the Universe who earlier sent down similar guidance to His truthful messengers, Ibrahim, Musa and 'Isa.

Having set the record straight with just two words—*al-Hayy* and *al-Qayyum*—which indicate that divinity of 'Uzayr, Maryam or 'Isa are self-contradictory, and therefore do not call for any theological discussion, now the Qur'an invites the People of the Book, essentially Jews and Christians, to compare the *da'wah* or the message of the Qur'an with the core message of their own earlier Divine Scripture, parts of which are retained in the Old and New Testaments.

At this point in time, another accusation is resolved by the Qur'an that it has not borrowed any material from the earlier Scriptures. The fact of the matter is that Allah sent down the same guidance of *tawhid*—of transcendent unity and uniqueness of the Creator and the Lord of the Universe—on Ibrahim, Musa and 'Isa. However, these original revealed teachings were not preserved by the Prophets' followers. Since the original message was not properly preserved, and only some fragments of the Divine revelation were reported in what exists today as their Scriptures, it was a logical necessity to send down the full message of guidance (*hidayah*) in the form of the uncorrupted and fully protected Qur'an.

Since the Qur'an is revealed by the very Law-Giver and Self-Subsisting Lord who earlier sent the same Truth, both the earlier and the last Messages should have resemblance and similarity in teachings, owing to the common source of these Scriptures.

POINT TO PONDER

The earlier Scriptures prohibited theft, unlawful sex, lying and killing; so, does the Qur'an as the Final Testament of Allah.

If earlier Scriptures declared theft, unlawful sex, lying and killing as prohibited, their mention in the Qur'an proves universality of truth and the Divine origin of the Qur'an. It is beside the point that the followers of earlier Scriptures edited and changed these commandments according to what suited them. Interestingly, these changes are recognized by the practicing Jewish and Christian scholars and by the editors of various versions of the earlier Scriptures. On the other hand, every single word and teaching of the Qur'an remains historically in its original form—both in the written as well as in the memorized form, by an unbroken chain of the millions of memorisers (*huffaz*) and reciters (*qurra'*) of the Qur'an—for the past fifteen centuries. The Qur'an refers to this phenomenon as evidence of its originality and the universality of its message and teachings.

The Qur'an puts it in simple words: "*Alif Lam Mim. Allah! There is no god but He—the Ever-Living, the Self-Subsisting. He has revealed this Book to you, setting forth the Truth and confirming the earlier Books, and He revealed the Torah and the Gospel before that, for the guidance of mankind; And He has also revealed the criterion (to distinguish the Truth from falsehood). A severe chastisement lies in store for those who deny the signs of Allah. Allah is Almighty; He is the Lord of Retribution. Nothing in the heavens and the earth is hidden from Allah. It is He who fashions you in the wombs as He wills. There is no god but He, the Almighty, the All-Wise.*" (Al 'Imran 3: 1–6)

The Qur'an as a Touchstone for Truth

Soon after referring to the Torah and the Gospel, the Qur'an highlights that it is *al-Furqan* (the touchstone for Truth and falsehood). The word *Furqan* comes from the root *f-r-q* which means "to separate, to make a distinction, to differentiate or to divide." The Qur'an, in this context, declares itself as the criterion of Truth and touchstone for what is right and wrong: "*Blessed is He who sent down al-Furqan to His servant...*" (al-Furqan 25: 1) The same word, *al-Furqan* is used with reference to the earlier scriptures, sent to guide earlier generations of people, at several places in the Qur'an, such as in *Surah al-Baqarah* 2: 53, *Surah Al 'Imran* 3: 4, and *Surah al-Anbiya'* 21: 48.

Due to the importance and impact of the Battle of Badr, the event was called *Yawm al-Furqan*, meaning the day which bears testimony to what was right and what was wrong. Naturally, a measure or criterion itself has to be exact; no more, no less than true. It is the Qur'an alone which can face all such tests of authenticity. This is why the Qur'an, as the uncorrupted Divine revelation, refers to the *original* teachings in the earlier Scriptures, even though these Scriptures were later corrupted by their followers.

After establishing the authenticity of the Qur'anic revelations, a reference is made to people who, even after knowing well the genuineness of this last Message, do not welcome it. Such people are warned of a chastisement waiting for them.

The opening statement that this guidance is from One Who is Self-Subsisting is reinforced by the verses that say that Allah alone is the Designer and Fashioner of everything including the creation of human beings.

Nothing is accidental. Everything is planned in a beautiful, balanced and most befitting manner.

Allah not only takes care of physical needs, but our spiritual needs too. Revealed guidance is an integral part of His balanced and beautiful grand plan. It is out of His Mercy that He did not leave human beings without providing them guidance on how to live a meaningful and wholesome life. As the Designer and the Architect, He alone, as the Originator, could provide a manual for the proper running of affairs in life.

Nevertheless, the People of the Book and the hypocrites had a habit of confusing the believers on various counts. One of their targets was the Qur'an itself. The Qur'an addresses a variety of topics and themes because it is the ultimate guidance containing the code for the whole of humanity. It contains legal commands, such as punishment for theft, murder, sexual offence, defamation etc. It also informs about matters beyond human perception and experience, like life in Paradise and Hell. It also mentions about things which are beyond human physical experience, a concept that the Qur'an terms as matters of the Unseen (*ghayb*). Even though these realities are not conceivable by human beings experientially, it does not mean that such realities do not exist. The Qur'an, even after mentioning such matters which are beyond the limitations of human experience, does not encourage believers to unnecessarily speculate on the nature of such matters. Yet, at the same time, it persuades all human beings to make use of their powers of reason, vision, audition and introspection to discover possible ways of solving human problems, in order to make life easy for them. In that sense, the Qur'an encourages scientific research, investigation, and development.

There is no conflict between the conduct of logical and scientific investigation and in-depth understanding (*tafaqquh*) of Islam. Though Islam does not agree with the assumption that only empirical reality is true, it repeatedly invites human beings to engage in investigation and research on all that exists for the benefit of human beings. It questions the ultimacy of reason and calls for research and development to be founded on Divine guidance (*wahi*).

The hypocrites and Jews in Madinah always looked for opportunities to create confusion and division within the Muslim community. The Qur'an refers to this phenomenon when it talks about substituting some earlier commandments given in the *Shari'ah* of Bani Isra'il by the final *Shari'ah* contained in the Qur'an and the Prophetic Sunnah. It also states that, with regards to the Islamic injunctions sent down over a course of twenty-three years, there was nothing wrong in the Creator modifying or substituting a directive with another command, if and when needed. The All-Knowing is fully aware of where and when a modification is needed, just as He is aware of the situations when there shall be no need for any modification or qualification of a command. Indeed, He is All-Knowing and All-Powerful. He is the Authority; neither is He subservient, at any time, to His own commands, nor is He subject to the laws He has made for mankind or for any of creation.

The Wisdom Behind *Naskh,* Qualification of *Ayat*

The issue of *naskh*, as a theme, has been a favourite topic of many of the exegetes (*mufassirun*). Eloquent and highly professional discussions have been made on this topic. For the purpose of our thematic understanding, those discussions are unnecessary because the *ayah* itself discourages spending time on matters of a non-empirical nature. However, why and how *naskh* takes place calls for a brief discussion. It is obvious from the *ayah* (Al 'Imran 3: 7) that the Qur'an wants believers to follow dedicatedly what is evident and clearly stated (*muhkam*) and to accept all matters which are beyond empirical experience (*mutashabihat*) as they remain an integral part of faith (*iman*). At the same time, in all matters that relate to human needs, the Qur'an wants the believers to conduct research on the implications of *muhkamat,* or the well-defined and evident rulings (*ahkam*) of the Qur'an. The *muhkamat* provide the basics, i.e., guidance in all social, economic, political, cultural and legal matters.

The meaning of *naskh,* which has been often translated as 'abrogation' or 'void', can be better understood as suggested by Raghib al-Isfahani, as 'qualification'. One example from the Qur'an can make the point clear, for example, the Qur'an mentions: "*They ask you [O Prophet] about liquor and games of chance. Say: 'In both these, there is great evil and some benefit for people—but their evil is greater than their benefit.'*" (al-Baqarah 2: 219) The Qur'an in another place qualifies this statement (for which some scholars use the term *naskh*) when it says: "*O believers! Do not draw near to the prayer while you are intoxicated until you know what you are saying.*" (al-Nisa' 4: 43) Both above statements are further qualified by a later command: "*O believers! Intoxicants, games of chance, idolatrous sacrifices at alters, and divining arrows are all abominations—the handiwork of Satan. So, turn wholly away from it so that you may be successful.*" (al-Ma'idah 5: 90)

This *ayah* of *Surah al-Ma'idah,* known as *ayah tahrim al-khamar,* qualifies the earlier two *ayat* or supersedes them. A similar phenomenon exists in *Surah al-Anfal* where the number of patient and persistent (*sabirin*) is reduced. It is mentioned: "*O Prophet! Rouse believers to fighting. If there be twenty of you who persevere, they shall vanquish two hundred; and if there be of you one hundred, they shall vanquish a thousand of those who disbelieve, for they are a people who lack understanding.*" (al-Anfal 8: 65)

The next *ayah* qualifies it when it mentions: "*Allah has now lightened your burden, for He found weakness in you. So, if there be one hundred of you who persevere, they shall vanquish two hundred; and if there be one thousand of you, they shall, by the leave of Allah, vanquish two thousand. Allah is with those who persevere.*" (al-Anfal 8: 66)

It must be noted that it is still within Allah's authority to make a total substitution of a command (*hukm*). For example, for over sixteen months,

Muslims prayed facing in the direction of Quds which was to the north of Madinah. But when the revelation: "*We see you often turning your face towards the sky; now We are turning you to the direction that will satisfy you. Turn your face towards the Holy Mosque, and wherever you are, turn your face towards it in prayer.*" (al-Baqarah 2: 144) came down, and the *Sahabah* heard a caller announcing this news while they were in the midst of offering the 'Asr prayer, they immediately turned their direction accordingly, towards the Masjid al-Haram in Makkah, which was to the south of Madinah. This command superseded the earlier permission to face Quds. When the Prophet Muhammad ﷺ was praying towards Quds, it was not his personal choice. It was by the command of Allah. Perhaps the wisdom in the command to pray towards Quds for over a year, was to let the Jewish community in Madinah realize that the Muslims respect the Sunnah of Prophet Dawud, which would provide one more common ground for developing a friendly atmosphere of dialogue. It also indicates Allah, who is the Legislator, has all authority to qualify an earlier command with a later *hukm* because of the changes to a situation.

As pointed out earlier, the Qur'an contains commands, directions and instructions on how to live a meaningful life. These commands deal with personal, familial, social, legal, political, economic and commercial, as well as cultural matters. These instructions are evident, clear and definite. No confusion or ambiguity is involved. For example, if the Qur'an declares to cut off the hand of a thief (male or female), it clearly refers to hand and not foot.

The Qur'an is a practical manual for making human life meaningful and purposeful. Those who deal with the Qur'anic knowledge (*ulum*) go into detailed discussions about *ayat* that deal with matters like what is meant by the hand of Allah, whether His throne (*'arsh*) is made of Gold or Crystal and with what speed angels can fly. All such speculative exercises are clearly prohibited by the Qur'an. The Qur'anic guidance is to make human life on Earth ethical, purposeful, and productive while serving Him and His servants as He wants. It is an ethical and moral manual of outcome-based conduct and behaviour. Its main concern is the ethical conduct of man in society. It discourages focussing on areas which are beyond the intellectual capacity of human beings. Allah says: "*He it is Who has revealed the Book to you. Among them there are the clear verses (muhkamat), and these are the core of the Book. Others are indistinct verses (mutashabihat). Those in whose hearts there is perversity, go about the part that is indistinct (mutashabih), seeking mischief and seeking to arrive at its meaning arbitrarily; although none knows their true meaning but Allah. But those firmly rooted in knowledge say: 'We believe in it; it is all from our Lord alone.' No one derives true admonition from anything except the people of understanding. They pray to Allah: 'Our Lord! Do not let our hearts swerve towards wickedness after You have guided us to the right way and bestow upon us Your Mercy for You are the Munificent Giver. Our Lord! One day You will surely gather all mankind together, a Day about (the coming of which) there is no doubt. Surely Allah never goes against His Promise.'*" (Al 'Imran 3: 7-9)

Sayyid Qutb makes a very simple yet remarkable observation on the *muhkamat* and *mutashabihat*: "In this brief passage, the *surah* uncovered the reality of those who swerve from the Truth. These people turn their backs on the facts stated with absolute clarity in the Qur'an, pursuing other Qur'anic statements which admit more than one explanation, in order to use them as a basis for their fabrication. It also shows the distinctive characters of those who truly believe in God and submit to Him, accepting everything they receive from Him without any doubt or argument."

This attitude of people towards the Qur'an, to pay no attention to the evident and clear statements (*nusus*), or to specific commandments and instructions, while picking up debates on matters beyond the realm of human perception and offering far-fetched interpretations, can be seen even among seemingly well-read Muslims. The use of the word *mutashabih*, meaning indistinct, does not allude to something that is irrelevant, unnecessary or confused. It simply refers to matters of fact which are beyond the empirical realm, such as the Face of Allah, which exists but details of which none can comprehend.

The Qur'an wants the believers to make use of reason, observation and experimentation in order to produce beneficial knowledge *(ilm al-nafi)* and avoid polemical discourses.

This does not reduce the importance of matters beyond empirical experience (*ghayb*); All such matters are to be taken as true and a part of a Muslim's belief.

Avoiding an Immoderate, Lavish and Prodigal Living

For some people, the purpose of life is enjoyment and fun. They love to live a lavish life, for which they are ready to even use unethical means. They prefer immediate worldly gains over the eternal life of pleasure. The Qur'an, on the other hand, wants believers to seek Allah's bounties for both this world and the Hereafter. It does not want us to pursue a glamorous life in this world at the cost of losing a life of eternal bliss in the Hereafter. Therefore, moderation and fairness (*'adl*) and austerity (*qana'ah*) are needed to attain a balanced personality, "*As for the unbelievers, neither their wealth nor their offspring will avail them in the least against Allah. They shall be the fuel of the Fire. [To them shall happen] the like of what happened to the people of Pharaoh, and those before them. They rejected Our signs (ayat) as false, so Allah seized them for their sins. Allah indeed is severe in punishment. [O Prophet!] Tell those who have disbelieved: 'You shall soon be overpowered and mustered to Hell—what an evil resting place.'*" (Al 'Imran 3: 10–12)

Success of Truth Over Falsehood

The Qur'an refers to the experience of Badr as a sign (*ayah*) of how a group of believers, around one-third the strength of the unbelievers and much less equipped than them, with Allah's help, defeated their opponent. The theme underscored is that it is sincerity (*ikhlas*), steadfastness in faith (*istiqamah*), and striving (*jihad*) in order to please Allah with persistence (*sabr*) which allows a group apparently less in quantity and equipment to overpower an enemy larger than them by several folds, "*You have already come across an instructive sign (ayah) in the two hosts that encountered each other in battle (at Badr); one host fighting in the way of Allah and the other that of unbelievers. They saw with their own eyes that one host was twice the number of the other. But (the result of the battle proves that) Allah succors with His victory whomever He wills. In this there is surely a lesson to all who have discerning eyes.*" (Al 'Imran 3: 13) The experience of Badr strengthened the faith of the *Sahabah* in their Lord, but the unbelievers did not learn any lesson from it. In fact, it only increased their enmity towards Islam and the Muslims.

Human beings (*insan*) are sometimes forgetful (*nisyan*), negligent and careless. The urge for power, authority, unlimited wealth, property and glamour often makes them forgetful of their duties towards the real Benefactor Who blesses them with the comforts in their lives. They realize their short-sightedness only when death approaches them suddenly. They find that neither their wealth nor their friends or relatives can be of any help to them; it is only their good deeds, done to please Allah alone, that can benefit them: "*People are naturally tempted by the love of women, children, treasures of gold, silver, horses of mark, cattle and plantations. These are the enjoyments in the life of the world; but with Allah lies a goodly abode to return to.*" (Al 'Imran 3: 14)

A unique style of the Qur'an is that it uses everyday examples to illustrate the common psyche of human beings. Human beings prefer an easy and comfortable life. Once they taste the pleasure of dealing with gold, of enjoying the most costly and modern automobiles, of living in big houses and so on, they long to have more such comforts and luxuries and forget to be grateful and loyal to the One Who provided them all these comforts in the first place. Islam does not want people to renounce worldly pleasures. It does not want them to live the life of a hermit. Rather, it wants its followers to maintain a balance and moderation (*'adl, qist, wasat*) and to develop an attitude of thankfulness (*hamd, shukr*) to the One Who has provided them these blessings. This can only be done by following His commands wholly and sincerely.

Every blessing and gift we receive from our Creator and Sustainer demands that we humble ourselves to Him—by observing the rights (*huquq*) due to Him, such as performing the prayers, fasting, etc; and by observing the *huquq* due to His creation, such as serving our parents, helping our relatives, neighbours , the elderly, those in need and spending to relieve people of their illnesses and pains.

This is how a believer prepares for success in the life Hereafter and simultaneously plays a constructive social role in this worldly life. For such people, who live a life of moderation and thankfulness to their Lord, their best possible reward awaits in Paradise. Good deeds done in this world lead to a life of permanent pleasure, comfort and enjoyment in the Hereafter.

Islam does not ask us to abandon Allah's blessings (*fadl*) upon us in the form of family, financial stability, good health, and children and friends. We can benefit from all these blessings but with gratefulness to Him. We must not become slaves to material needs and make compromises in our obedience to our Master's directions: "*Say [O Prophet]: 'Shall I tell you of things better than these? For the God-fearing (ittaqaw), they will have with their Lord, Gardens beneath which rivers flow; there they will abide forever, will have chaste spouses and the pleasure of Allah.' Allah thoroughly observes His servants. These are ones who pray: 'Our Lord! We have believed, so forgive our sins and keep us safe from the chastisement of the Fire.' [It is they] who are patient, truthful, obedient, spend [in the way of Allah] and implore Allah's forgiveness before daybreak.*" (Al 'Imran 3: 15–17)

Islam, as a faith, implies full and active participation in professional activities alongside the realization of justice (*'adl*), truth (*sidq*), steadfastness (*istiqamah*), patience (*sabr*), and making generous contributions (*infaq* and *sadaqat*) in the way of Allah. For such persons, the Qur'an promises excellent and generous rewards in the life Hereafter.

Tawhid, as the foundation and anchor of faith, is a major theme in the Qur'an. *Surah al-Ikhlas* which is also known as the "*surah* of *tawhid*" in this sense covers one-third of the faith and the Islamic teachings. The other two major teachings include belief in the finality of the Prophethood, of the Seal of the Prophets (*Khatam al-Nabiyyin*), i.e., Prophet Muhammad ﷺ, and belief in the Day of Judgement and the Afterlife. The Qur'an repeatedly underscores the centrality and impact of *tawhid* on the life of a believer. *Tawhid* should be instilled in every aspect of life, be it thought, feelings or behaviour. The guiding force remains seeking the pleasure (*rida*) of Allah.

When we perform a well-thought, reasoned-out, cognitive action or when we have an instant emotional response, it is usually attributed to emotional intelligence. The deciding factor, Islamically however, is neither purely rational nor emotional; rather, it is convictional and ethical, and it stems from a single question: Is this act going to please Allah or not? This is precisely the role of *tawhid, taqwa* (God-consciousness) and *khashiyah* (awareness due to the sense of being in His presence) which I call ethical intelligence.

Needless to say, every single thing in the heavens and the earth and the whole universe bears witness to this fact. In other words, all that is in the universe, living or non-living, follows *tawhid* and bears witness and obedience to Allah alone.

"Allah Himself bears witness that there is no god but He, and so do the angels and those endowed with knowledge (qa'im bi al-qist) bear witness in truth and justice that there is no god but He, the Almighty the All-Wise." (Al 'Imran 3: 18) This *ayah* beautifully reconfirms a believer's conviction that there is no God other than Allah and to Him belongs all power, authority, command and grip on everything in the universe. Therefore, He alone deserves obedience and to be served (*'ubudiyyah*). Not only is every single object in the created world evidence to His supremacy and power; He Himself bears witness to this fact too.

To bear witness to Allah's Transcendence and Unity is viewed here as the fair, just and reasoned attitude of a believer. Therefore, the term used for such a believer is one who has settled at *qist* or *'adl*.

The terminology *qist* means to be equal and fair; *qistas* means "a measuring scale". The people of *qist* therefore means those who are not tilted, biased, partial or partisan. Serving Allah alone, thus, becomes the imperative when a person thinks and acts objectively, and not subjectively.

The Uniqueness, Unity and Authority of Allah is such an evident truth which cannot be overlooked by any sensible person. If human beings only look critically to their own existence or that of the universe around them, they will realize that the existence of balance (*'adl*), beauty (*husn*) and the benefits human beings enjoy are not possible without the Compassionate Being, who disregards the shortcomings of His servants and, despite their weaknesses, continues to bestow His favours on them. Not only human intellect and intuition bears witness to this truth, but all the Messengers of Allah bear witness to this Truth, and it is reflected in their teachings, practices, and in the Scriptures which they delivered to their people. This is such a self-evident, paramount and transcendent reality that the Lord of all that exists, Himself, endorses it as the unparalleled truth.

Invitation to Use Reason (*Ta'aqul*), Critical Thinking, Contemplation (*Tafakkur*), and Introspection (*Tadabbur*)

The Qur'an persuades its readers to think logically and to correlate observation, historic heritage and experience, in order to discover truth and reality. Like a six-year-old girl who wants to understand why stars twinkle and why different types of flowers, say rose and jasmine, smell differently when both are watered in one and the same flowerpot; every human being is expected to search for answers to questions like: Who is the Creator of this beautiful and intricate universe? Does life end with the physical death of a person or is there another realm of life? What is the purpose of life? And what is meant by a successful life?

The Qur'an invites human beings to explore and investigate into their own process of creation. It points out how a human being is developed from a congealed clot of blood, which contains the complete information of their personality traits, and at a micro level, carries the map of their whole body. This complex process of human development cannot take place without being caused by an Originator, the Most Knowledgeable Lord of the universe, it is easy for One Who is Transcendent and Perfect to design and fashion a perfect human being. Allah refers to this when He says: "*Surely, We created human beings (insan) in the best mould.*" (al-Tin 95: 4) In other words, since the creation of the human being is in the best (*ahsan*) form, it simply means that human beings are not a result of a blind process of trial and error, or an autonomous biological evolution, but the work of a well-conceived mapping by the Most Wise Creator. This evidence from within, the witnessing (*shahadah*) of our own soul (*nafs*), testifies to the creativity of the Most Kind and the Praiseworthy, and to the invalidity of the so-called autonomous biological evolution of man.

We also see that the creation of everything around us is in pairs (in terms of the opposite sex) whether among plants, flowers and vegetation, in the animal world or among human beings. It also offers evidence of the One Who exists by Himself but, in order to have a sustainable world, has created everything in pairs at a universal level.

Human history provides evidence on the role of ethical and moral laws which operate across the board, irrespective of colour, race or sex. The Qur'an in this respect, questions the Jewish claim that the people from the seed of Dawud [David] are the chosen race. It substitutes the concept of superiority due to race, colour or ethnicity with ethical and moral conduct (*taqwa*, *birr*, *'amal salih*) as the basis of superiority. Historical remains of the highly developed societies of Yemen, Syria and Egypt are evidence to how a society's moral decay led to its fall and destruction. Oppression, exploitation and disorder (*taghut*, *zulm*, *fitnah* and *fasad*), according to the Divine principles, are what bring about the decline of a society. Therefore, it is only ethical and moral change that can remove injustice and exploitation from a society and establish *ma'ruf* and good in it.

This phenomenon is also evidenced by the Scriptures of the world religions. All Scriptures, even unwritten scriptures of several African religions, invite their followers to obey and call for help from the Ultimate King, Ruler and Owner. The name of their deity may differ, but they all share a common belief in a Supreme Being. The Qur'an calls this a unity in *shara'iy* or Divine guidance. From Adam to the Final Messenger ﷺ, all Prophets of Allah called the people to obey Allah alone, which is undeniable evidence of *tawhid* as the original faith of humanity.

Besides the belief in the Ultimate Creator, all revealed religions—Judaism, Christianity, and Islam—have a common belief regarding the existence of angels who carry out orders from Allah and unconditionally obey and serve Him.

It is to this backdrop that the Qur'an mentions that Allah Himself affirms His transcendent attributes and bears witness (*shahadah*) to His power, knowledge, and the nurturing of His creatures. When we use the word "witness" it includes visual evidence as well as rational and circumstantial evidence. Since all possible evidences converge to a single point that Allah is the only Authority in the universe, a logical consequence is that He alone deserves to be obeyed, worshipped, and praised for His love, kindness, compassion and unfailing care of all human beings and creatures.

POINT TO PONDER

Anyone who understands the meaning of *'adl* and believes in Allah to be *al-'Adil* (the Most Fair) cannot perceive that a person who is innocent and has not committed any wrong, should be allowed to be hanged for the sins and wrongs of others. That would be a total violation of the Divine principle of *'adl.* Therefore, by implication, the so-called sacrifice of 'Isa for the sins of humankind (also the so-called fall and inheriting of sin by human beings) is a logical contradiction and is contrary to Allah's justice and equity.

Realization of *Tawhid* as a Matter of Faith, and Way of Life

One who follows the *tawhidic* way of life makes a conscious effort to liberate oneself from the grip of prevalent customs and the deviant ways of people who divide their lives usually in two or more distinct domains: a domain of spirituality, religiosity and piety manifested in their regular prayers, fasting, payment of zakah, and performance of hajj and *'umrah* on one hand; and another domain in which they serve the interests of the global capitalist order and secular democracy, enjoy unrestricted greed for power, wealth and fame and seek pleasure and fun as their core objectives in life. Many people observe this dualism and assume that a successful life means maintaining a balance between the so-called material and spiritual domains.

The Qur'an and the Prophetic Sunnah, on the contrary, ask believers to enter Islam in totality (*udkhilu fi al-silmi kaffah*). A *tawhidic* way of life recognizes no separation between the religious and secular spaces. Islam demands all human activities whether economic, political, legal, social or personal, to be performed in order to please the Ultimate Master and Sovereign. *Tawhid* in other words is a natural and cosmic truth; everything that exists, animate or inanimate, by its very nature observes and follows it. Islam is the conscious realization of this *tawhidic* reality within human transactions in socio-economic, cultural and political activities.

With these dimensions of *tawhid*, the Qur'an moves to a simple and comprehensive statement of the fact that invitation to *tawhid*—a conscious and willful acceptance of servitude to Allah—is not only a rational demand, but essentially the common basis of the message (*da'wah*) of all Messengers of Allah. The Qur'an introduces *tawhid* in its pristine form. The true way of life, therefore, can only be one in which human beings eliminate following multiple gods. Such a way of life gets rid of dualism and follows only the one true guidance coming from the One true Lord. The *ayah* continues: "*The true din [way of life] with Allah is Islam. The people of the Book adopted many different ways rather than follow the true way of Islam even after the knowledge of Truth had reached them, and this merely to commit excesses against one another. Let him who refuses to follow the ordinances and directions of Allah know that surely Allah is swift in His reckoning.*" (Al 'Imran 3: 19)

Unity and Variety

Many religious scholars in the field of interfaith dialogue, albeit with good intention, claim that since all faiths talk about truth, peace and love, the presence of truth, peace and love in different faiths means that truth is pluralistic. A comparative study of the different faiths, however, will indicate that each faith has a different meaning attached to each of these concepts. Similarly, most of the religions believe in an ultimate deity called by different names, such as 'the Universal Soul', 'Father', and so on. The fact of the matter is that each religion interprets its deity in a different way, and quite often their god carries conflicting and diverse attributes. Therefore, all faces of God cannot be ultimately true, same and authentic. Duplicity of gods causes conflict and contradiction in life. It is faith in the One and Only Creator, God, Allah, that can bring unity in life.

The Qur'an approaches this issue, not only from an analytical perspective, but also from a historical one. It refers to the original faith of Ibrahim, the patriarch, in whose lineage Ya'qub, Musa [Moses] and 'Isa [Jesus] came to revive the Abrahamic faith. It declares: "*Abraham was neither a Jew nor a Christian; he was a Muslim wholly devoted to God, and he certainly was not amongst the polytheists [those who associated others with Allah in His Divinity].*" (Al 'Imran 3: 67) Ibrahim called his people to follow uncompromising Unity of the Lord, Allah. The Prophet Muhammad ﷺ revived the pristine *tawhid*, the faith of his great-great-grandfather, Ibrahim, with complete honesty.

Since the Qur'an addresses Ibrahim as none other than a Muslim, the true *din*, the right way of life, is in fact the pristine faith of Ibrahim. Therefore, historically as well as conceptually, the Abrahamic way of life (*din*) is the only authentic *din*. Those who deviate from this, the Qur'an mentions, shall suffer in the life Hereafter, whereas those who follow the original faith of Ibrahim, shall enjoy the pleasures of *Jannah*.

The Culture of Freedom of Faith and Unity in Variety

One major theme of the Qur'an, across the board, from *Surah al-Fatihah* to *Surah al-Nas* is to develop a proper link with the Kind, Merciful, and Supreme Being Allah, the One Who is not despotic and oppressive, yet carries boundless, unrestricted power and authority. He is the Merciful (*al-Rahman*), the All-Compassionate (*al-Rahim*), the Forgiving (*al-Ghafur*), the Pardoning (*al-'Afuww*) and the Most Loving (*al-Wadud*). He is keen to see His servants observe fairness, kindness, thankfulness and dutifulness. Therefore, He never leaves His servants without showing them the True Path (*sirat al-mustaqim*) to ultimate success, and of attainment and felicity (*al-fawz wa al-falah wa al sa'adah*). If His servant calls Him, He responds, and if His servant moves one step towards Him, He moves ten steps towards them. We must take the first step in order to get close to Him and seek the Right Way and build an awareness of the Truth. The Qur'an facilitates this on at least three levels.

First, the Qur'an invites its readers to examine their own existence; how the process of human development takes place, right from the union of two chromosomes—not visible to the human eye, yet carrying the complete genetic information of a human being—to the completion of the whole bodily system, made fully functional even before physical birth takes place. We are urged to ponder if such an intricate process of development could take place without an All-Powerful and All-Aware Designer and Creator.

Second, the Qur'an asks its readers to critically study the history of humankind in order to learn what causes the rise and fall of societies and civilizations, and to take lessons from it. Third, the role model of the Final Messenger of Allah ﷺ, fully preserved in his authentic practice (Sunnah) and recorded with great care in the Hadith literature, provides a living example of how *tawhid* can be translated into personal behaviour within social conduct, governance and within the economic and political realms, "*There has come to you a Messenger of Allah, from among yourselves, who is distressed by the losses you sustain, who is ardently desirous of your welfare, and is tender and merciful to those who believe.*" (al-Tawbah 9: 128) The most prominent quality of the Prophet ﷺ mentioned in the Qur'an is his mercy (*rahmah*). He was sent by Allah Who is *al-Rahman* and *al-Rahim*, the Merciful, the Beneficent with a message of hope, mercy and forgiveness for any lapses made by us, human beings. The Prophet ﷺ was eager to save and protect people from punishment and to show them the path of success which leads to eternal bliss and satisfaction.

The Qur'an reminds us that the *din,* the way of life, enumerated by all the Messengers of Allah is one and the same. All of them invited their people to obedience to only One Allah and they never claimed any share in His Divinity, "*We raised a Messenger in every community (to tell them): 'Serve Allah and shun all the evil ones (al-taghut).*'" (al-Nahl 16: 36) This was the *din* of Ibrahim and 'Isa, "*You have a good example in Abraham and those with him, when they said to their people: 'We totally dissociate ourselves from you and from the deities that you worship instead of Allah. We renounce you, and there has come to be enmity and hatred between us and you until you believe in Allah, the One True God.*'" (al-Mumtahnah 60: 4) 'Isa also preached the very same message: "*Those who say, 'Allah is the Messiah, son of Mary,' have certainly fallen into disbelief; whereas the Messiah [himself] said: 'O Children of Israel! Worship Allah Who is my Lord and your Lord.' Allah has forbidden Paradise to those who associate others with Him [in His Divinity] and their refuge shall be the Fire. And the wrongdoers will have no helpers.*" (al-Ma'idah 5: 72)

The Qur'an reminds Bani Isra'il and the followers of 'Isa that the Islamic message is not different from what Ibrahim and 'Isa delivered. Therefore, the Messenger ﷺ is commissioned to invite all human beings towards the Final Message of Allah, the Qur'an, while no use of force is allowed for conversion.

On the other hand, the Crusades in the eleventh and twelfth centuries were waged by the Church, according to Church history, to convert the Jews and the Muslims. The same was done by the champions of colonialism who used their economic, political and educational strategies to marginalize the native religions and culture, particularly that of the Muslims. The Qur'an advises the Messenger ﷺ to let people know fully about the Truth and to let them use their independent judgement on whether to embrace Islam or not. The same policy of "no compulsion" was followed by the Muslims when they ruled over a major part of the world for over eight centuries in Spain, Africa, Asia, the Middle East and the South and Southeast Asia.

The Qur'an mentions: "*But if they argue with you (O Prophet), say: 'I have submitted my whole being to Allah, and so have those who follow me.' And ask those who were given the Scripture and the unlettered (ummiyyin): 'Have you also submitted (to Allah)?' If they have submitted to Him they are indeed on the Right Way, but if they turn away from submitting to Allah, then your duty is merely to deliver the Message. Allah is All-Seeing of His servants.*" (Al 'Imran 3: 20)

It is important to note that the Qur'an traces the origin of Islam to the faith and mission of Ibrahim who was the foremost precursor of *tawhid*, much before the development of Rabbinic Judaism and Paulian Christianity. Islam, therefore, does not borrow its teachings from Jewish or Christian sources. In fact, its central theme of obedience to the One and Only Allah, appears common with the Jewish and Christian beliefs. Second, the Qur'an also elaborates that the true *din* or way of life with Allah is only Islam as delivered by the Final Messenger ﷺ of Allah. Therefore, all those who believe in the One and Only Originator of mankind and in the Day of Judgement are invited to embrace Islam. While reminding the people of the Book about their original faith, the Qur'an also addresses the unlettered (*ummiyin*). They may not have received a book but they too were approached by Allah's messenger, because Allah has not left anyone without a warner and guide.

At the same time, the Qur'an also warns those who have deviated from the Right Way, like the Bani Isra'il, about the consequences of refusing to follow the Lord's directions, "*Indeed, those who deny the signs of Allah, slay the Prophets unjustly, and kill those who enjoin justice—give them the glad tidings of a grievous chastisement. They are the people whose works have gone to waste both in this world and in the world to come. They have none to come to their help.*" (Al 'Imran 3: 21–22)

Knowing full well the psychology of the People of the Book, their continuous tricky ways and their consistent evading and avoiding clear injunctions of their own Scripture, the Prophet ﷺ keeps on inviting them to the Right Way, to the Qur'an which endorses the original teachings of Ibrahim, Isma'il, Ishaq, Ya'qub, Musa and 'Isa, and also corrects confusions made by their priests. The optimism of the Prophet ﷺ, his consistency and pursuance, is exemplary for *da'wah* workers. He even prays for those who reject his message and for their progeny to one day enter into the fold of Islam. Aside from inviting the People of the Book, the Prophet ﷺ also invites the progeny of Isma'il, who were called *ummi* (literally, a person who did not go through formal institutional schooling), to embrace Islam. Though called *ummi*, they had a refined literary tradition of excellence in poetry, and were recognized for global trading and the art of warfare. The word *ummi* or being unlettered, simply meant that they were not carriers of a Divine Book, as proudly claimed by the Bani Isra'il.

While inviting the People of the Book, the Qur'an also discusses the historicity of their Scripture—that in its present form, it contains only a small portion of its original teachings. The Qur'anic revelation, on the other hand, is fully preserved in its original version and provides a complete code of life. Therefore, based on common sense, it is to their own advantage to welcome Islam which revives the original faith and teachings of Ibrahim, Ishaq, Isma'il, Musa and 'Isa , "*Have you not noticed those who were given a portion of the Book [the Jews and the Christians]? Whenever their learned men are summoned to the Book of Allah to judge the difference among them, a party of them turns away in aversion. This is because they say: 'The Fire of Hell shall not touch us except for a limited number of days.' Their false beliefs which they have forged have deluded them in their faith. How then, will they fare when We shall gather them altogether to witness the Day about which there is no doubt—when every human being shall be paid in full for what he has done, and none shall be wronged!*" (Al 'Imran 3: 23–25)

Bani Isra'il's Delusions

The above *ayat* refer to one of the self-deceptions of the People of the Book, which posit that, due to being a "chosen" people, they will receive special treatment in the Hereafter, and that even if they must go through punishment for their unethical behaviour, the Hellfire will not touch them except for a short and temporary duration. The Qur'an questions their self-claimed preferential treatment in the life Hereafter, because Allah is extremely Just (*al-'Adil*) and people shall be judged by Him only on the basis of their beliefs and deeds, not their genealogy.

The Qur'an tells us that the Bani Isra'il lost its leadership role due to its daring and continuous violations of its own Scriptures; whereas the Muslim community, due to its conscious acceptance of serving Allah alone, was given this noble role and responsibility. The prayer that follows has a tacit message on why a change in leadership becomes necessary: "*Say (O Prophet): 'O Allah, Lord of the dominion! You bestow dominion on whomever You please and take away dominion from whomever You please; and You exalt whom You please and abase whom You please. In Your hand is all good. Surely You are All-Powerful. You cause night to pass into the day and the day to pass into the night. You bring forth the living out of the dead and You bring the dead out of the living, and You grant livelihood to whomever You will, beyond all reckoning.'*" (Al 'Imran 3: 26–27)

This beautiful *du'a'* carries an indication that the leadership role of Bani Isra'il was going to be transferred to the Muslim *ummah*; and that Bani Isra'il, due to their ungratefulness and rebellious attitude, was going to be relieved of the leadership role. Here, this leadership role is called a *fadl* or blessing of Allah, which He bestows upon whomsoever He wills. But those who are conferred this favour, shoulder a huge responsibility to not only act with responsibility and restraint (*amanah, sidq, diyanah*), but to also put all their energy towards realizing the establishment (*iqamah*) of Allah's *din* in every domain of their life. This gift is called *rizq*—a term which is normally used to refer to food needed for sustainability, it actually has much wider implications: Guidance (*hidayah*) is *rizq*, and so is revelation (*wahi*). Without them, human beings may live a biological life but will lack the essence of living due to their oblivion of concepts such as God-conciousness (*taqwa*), righteous deeds (*'amal salih*), mode of worship (*'ubudiyyah*), and testimony of truth, patience, and steadfastness (*shahadah* of *haqq*, *sabr* and *istiqamah*). None can progress and sustain a meaningful life without the *rizq* of *wahi* and *hidayah*. Therefore, Allah may reward with *rizq*, in its wider meaning, to whomever He selects because of their servitude to Him. Their love of Allah has no other meaning than total obedience, *ta'ah*, *ta'abbud*, *taslim* and *taharah* of *nafs*.

A similar message is given by the Qur'an in another place: "*And pray: 'My Lord, cause me to enter wherever it be with Truth, and cause me to exit wherever it be with Truth, and support me with all authority (sultah) from Yourself.'*" (*al-Isra'* 17: 80) This *du'a'* is reported to have been made by the Prophet Muhammad ﷺ in the context of his migration to Madinah. The *du'a'* clearly states that he was not seeking refuge as a fugitive but he desired to leave his hometown, where the House of Allah was located, with dignity, honour and truth, and also desired to enter the new habitation with humbleness, gratitude, strength and glorification of Allah, in order to establish Allah's Authority, Power and Sovereignty in the land.

The Ethics of Intercommunal Relations

Islam is essentially a social faith where complementarity and fraternity is observed in most matters of life, including acts of worship (*'ibadat*). Most obligatory *'ibadat* that are prescribed upon the believers—irrespective of their colour and race—are to be performed congregationally. The five daily prayers are to be performed in congregation in the mosque. In Ramadan, the month of fasting, every believer across the globe fasts during the prescribed duration and performs late-night *tarawih* prayers collectively. Similarly, hajj and *'umrah* are performed in unison. This indicates that the Muslim community has its foundations in brotherhood (*ukhuwah*), collaboration in good (*ta'awu 'ala al-birr*) and counselling (*nasihah*).

An Islamic society, in a sense, is a pluralistic society where non-Muslim citizens live and contribute in the economic and technological spheres. The Qur'an provides clear guidelines on mutual relations among the believers and the non-Muslims, as well as with the hypocrites. The Qur'an accounts for situations in which the Muslims may be a majority as well as situations where they may be a minority. In both cases *ijtima'iyyah*, living a community life, helping each other in good (*ma'ruf*) and dissociating from all unethical behaviours (*munkar*) is demanded by their faith.

From day one, Islam was never a personal or a land-locked faith like Hinduism or Zoroastrianism. Madinah had both believers as well as Jews and hypocrites as its citizens. The state was an ideological state and not a theocracy with a privileged group to rule and exercise certain "religious" functions. Every citizen enjoyed basic human rights. Although, because it was an ideological state and one that had in it a Muslim-majority population, the state was naturally responsible for the implementation of the Qur'anic and the Sunnah legislations. This, in no way, infringed on the complete religious freedom that non-Muslim citizens enjoyed.

Interfaith Relationship

Non-Muslims in an Islamic state enjoy full security and freedom. But the experience with the Jewish community in Madinah was not pleasant. As soon as the Prophet ﷺ arrived in Madinah (at the invitation of the believers from the Khazraj and Aws tribes), a covenant was signed between the Prophet ﷺ and the Jewish tribes living in the surroundings of Madinah, known as the "Covenant of Madinah" (i.e. *Mithaq al-Madinah*). Through this covenant, the Jewish tribes were bound to jointly defend the city of Madinah and accept the Prophet ﷺ as the final judge in all matters. But from day one, the Jewish community remained involved in subversive activities in collaboration with the polytheists of Makkah. The battles of Badr and Uhud exposed their alliance with the *mushrikin* of Makkah. After the successful campaign of *al-Ahzab* (in the fifth year of Hijrah), it became evident that the Islamic state of Madinah was here to stay. Now it was time to review the *Mithaq al-Madinah*. It is in this context the Qur'an advised the Muslim community not to take the non-Muslims as allies anymore. Believers are asked to trust and develop mutual dependence only on the believers.

"*The believers may not take the unbelievers for their allies (awliya') in preference to the believers. Whoever does this, has nothing to do with Allah—unless he does so in order to protect himself from their wrongdoings. Allah warns you to beware of Him for to Allah is the ultimate return. Say [O Prophet]: 'Whether you conceal what is in your hearts or disclose it, Allah knows it. Allah knows all that is in the heavens and in the earth, and He has power over everything.' The Day is approaching when every soul shall find itself confronted with whatever good it has wrought. It will then wish that there be a wide space between it and the Day. Allah warns you to beware of Him, He is Most Tender toward His servants.*" (Al 'Imran 3: 28–30)

The word used in the Qur'an is *awliya'*. Its singular form, *wali*, means helper, benefactor, friend, supporter, a close associate, patron, protector, guardian or sponsor. In its popular understanding, the word *wali* is used for a pious person. Therefore, the word *wali* often refers to a saint, someone known for piety, whereas those who develop friendship with Satan are called *awliya' al-shaytan.* Within the popular ideology of Sufism, a *wali* is considered saintly, pious and nearly immune or *ma'sum*, one who is protected from committing wrong and may also save people from chastisement. Such persons become central figures among the masses as symbols of godliness. To support this heretic view, some *ayat* of the Qur'an such as: '*Surely, the friends of Allah have nothing to fear, nor shall they grieve. [They are] the ones who believe and are God-fearing,*' (Yunus 10: 62–63) are interpreted out of context. In reality though, the *ayat* explicitly define "friends of Allah" as only those who have *iman* and *taqwa* and does not refer at all to those who claim hereditary sainthood or spirituality.

> The word *awliya'* of Allah is defined in the *ayah* as persons who have total faith in Allah and have ethical and moral conduct (*taqwa*). It does not refer to the popular concept of "friends of Allah" who live like a hermit or, on the other hand, live a princely life under the pretext of holiness and spirituality. Friends of Allah are those who stand for truth, justice, fairness with humility, *taqwa*, *sabr* and *istiqamah*.

When the Qur'an talks about not taking unbelievers as *awliya'*, or allies, it refers specifically to those who, like the *mushrikun* of Makkah or the *munafiqun* of Madinah, had traditional enmity toward Islam. Naturally, a people who wanted to destabilize the state of Madinah, who tried their best to harm the Prophet ﷺ, and who were, at all times, conspiring with the neighbouring Jewish tribes of Madinah and with the Makkans, could not be trusted as sincere *awliya'*. However, if any one of them genuinely embraced Islam, the same person became a dear brother or sister in faith. The dislike and distrust towards the polytheists were due to the pollution in their ideology or *shirk*, and had nothing to do with their ethnicity, colour or race.

The Qur'an further elaborates: "*O Believers! Do not take the unbelievers as your allies in preference to the believers. Do you wish to offer Allah a clear proof of guilt against yourselves?*" (al-Nisa' 4: 144); "*O Believers! Do not make friends with My enemies and your enemies, showing them affection whereas they have spurned the Truth that has come to you. They expelled the Messenger and yourselves [out of Makkah] for no other reason than that you believe in Allah, Your Lord. If you have left [your homes and have come forth] to struggle in My way and to seek My good pleasure [then do not take them as allies], disclosing secrets to the pagans out of affection for them, although I know well whatever you do, be it secretly or publicly. And whomsoever of you does so has indeed strayed far away from the Straight Path. If they could overcome you, they would act as your foes and would hurt you by their hands and tongues and would love to see you become unbelievers.*" (al-Mumtahnah 60: 1–2)

These *ayat* refer to the attitude of the hypocrites, the *mushrikin,* and the Jewish tribes of Madinah with whom the major tribes of Ansar, i.e., the Aws and Khazraj, had a long history of alliance. But once the Aws and Khazraj entered into the fold of Islam, the Jewish tribes disregarded their old alliance and did not hesitate to harm the Ansar; while the Ansar, due to their humbleness, always had a soft corner towards them. The Qur'an advises the believers to be careful, to identify their covert enemies, and not to be deceived by the duplicity of the unbelievers and hypocrites.

The application of these *ayat*, like the bulk of other *ayat*, is not limited to the events that took place between the believers and the Makkans or the hypocrites in Madinah. At a universal level, the Muslims are advised to be selective in choosing friends. The idea is to develop self-reliance and ideological affinity. Those who are known for their materialistic and expansionistic global policies, in all sincerity, cannot be considered as *awliya'* or friends. They use alliances for their own hegemonic designs. Muslims should seek only Allah's help and establish their economic, scientific and political independence. They should not allow the imperialist powers to exploit them in the name of globalization.

The Qur'an offers a solid basis of social solidarity, i.e., *ukhuwah*, by inculcation of *iman*, *taqwa* and *'amal salih* among the Muslims. But this socialization alone will not benefit anyone on the Day of Judgement if a person is not obedient to Allah and the Prophet ﷺ, "*As for those who believe and do good deeds, He will reward them in full and will give them much out of His bounty. But those who have been disdainful and arrogant, He will subject them to a painful chastisement; and they will find for themselves neither any guardian [wali] nor helper [nasir] apart from Allah.*" (al-Nisa' 4: 173) The same message is conveyed in several places: "*And warn with this [revealed message] those who fear that they shall be mustered to their Lord, that there will be none apart from Allah to act as their protector [wali] and intercessor (shafi'); then maybe they will become God-fearing [yattaqun].*" (al-An'am 6: 51) That no one can help, recommend or intercede on the Day of Judgement is explicitly clear in, not one, but several places in the Qur'an, "*Lo! To Allah [alone] belongs the sincere devotion [din]. As for those who have taken other than Allah for their guardians [awliya'], [they say]: 'We worship them only that they bring us nearer to Allah.' Allah will judge between them concerning what they differ about. Verily, Allah does not guide whoever persists in lying and disbelief.*" (al-Zumar 39: 3)

No Intercession

All of these Qur'anic references, and many more, elaborate the incorrectness of popular belief that a *wali* can intercede for a person in front of Allah. Allah wants every believer to approach Him directly without any intermediary: "*When my servants ask you [O Prophet] about Me, tell them I am indeed near. I hear and answer the caller whenever he calls Me. Let them respond [with obedience] to Me and believe in Me perhaps they will be guided aright.*" (al-Baqarah 2: 186) The Qur'an further says in another place: "*Surely, We have created man and We know the prompting of his heart and We are nearer to him than even his jugular vein.*" (Qaf 50: 16) Allah wants His servants to call Him directly: "*Your Lord said, 'Pray to Me and I will respond to you....'*"

(al-Mu'min 40: 60) With these self-evident, direct instructions from Allah that He is nearer to one than his/her own jugular vein, and that He not only listens but accepts His servants' prayers, there remains no room for approaching Allah indirectly through intermediaries. Allah is closer to a person than their own jugular vein, in terms of His Knowledge. The idea of Him being physically present inside of His creation, whether that is on Earth (as the Christians claim for Jesus) or within a human (as followers of monistic religions believe), doesn't befit the Lord's Majesty and Divinity.

Kind and Hospitable Attitude Towards Unbelievers

Islamic *da'wah* considers all non-believers as potential Muslims; therefore, one is not supposed to totally cut social relations with them. The Qur'an expects believers to deal with non-believers in the most polite and ethical manner, with dignity and co-operation, and to help them whenever a genuine need arises. The Prophetic example is the authentic source of guidance in this respect. He used to sincerely help the non-Muslims even when they were unfriendly to him, such as in the case of the famine in Makkah when he generously offered them food supplies. The Islamic state is, therefore, obliged to take care of the needs of the non-Muslim citizens, to protect their lives, honour, property, family environment and to provide the facilities needed for their worship.

Similarly, non-Muslims can always be engaged with when it comes to technical and professional matters where specific skills or specialization is required. We know that when migrating from Makkah to Madinah, the Prophet ﷺ hired a non-Muslim who was more knowledgeable about the travel routes than others who were believers. Islam wants its followers to be just, and allows all citizens of an Islamic state to contribute their share in building a fair and peaceful order. Although, in strategic areas, it is the believers alone that could be entrusted specific responsibilities.

Holding of Key Positions

The issue of a non-Muslim holding a strategic political office needs to be understood in light of the nature of an Islamic state. An Islamic state is ideological and, by its very constitution, requires a person who has full commitment, ownership and loyalty to its ideology, and is competent to understand and implement the *Shari'ah* injunctions as an obligation, to be the one to run the office. Just as the idea of the appointment of a non-socialist person within a socialist republic office is illogical, so too is the idea of a non-Muslim's appointment within the strategic office of an Islamic state. In an Islamic ideological state, its policy planners and implementors should have undisputed loyalty to Islam, to the Prophet ﷺ and to the Islamic code of life, the *Shari'ah*.

On the other side, it is also incorrect to think that any Muslim within an Islamic state can be appointed to strategic positions of office. This is like taking the example of a medical school where not every MBBS or MD can undertake teaching every medical speciality, and where general practice professionals cannot simply be appointed as professor of surgery, gynecology, or cardiology. Similarly, only those Muslims who meet the basic requirements of honesty and trustworthiness (*amanah*), truth (*sidq*), fairness (*'adl*), and observance of obligatory prayers and conformity with the Prophetic Sunnah, qualify to be considered for a public office. A person, though Muslim, but known for corruption cannot be a candidate for public office.

In an Islamic state, only those Muslims who have the capacity to understand the spirit of the Qur'anic and Sunnah legislations can operate the system. In a Muslim majority country, for example, in Pakistan, as specified in the country's constitution, the President or Prime Minister should be a Muslim with commitment to the Qur'an and the Sunnah. Only then, one can ensure implementation of Islamic injunctions. It is not a pre-requisite for the person to be a graduate of a religious seminary or to belong to a particular legal school or *madhhab*. In a 97% Muslim majority country, democratic norms demand a leader who represents them and can protect their faith, culture and traditions. Needless to say, an Islamic state guarantees full religious and cultural freedom to its non-Muslim citizens.

Obedience to the Prophet ﷺ

The Muslim society is founded on the universal principles of Truth (*Haqq*), i.e., the realization of Allah's Sovereignty on His land and the unconditional following of the Prophet's example. A believer cannot differentiate between obedience to Allah and following in the footsteps of His Final Messenger ﷺ. This is not a view of scholars, but a command of Allah.

In other words, not only is following the practice of the Prophet ﷺ, i.e., the Sunnah, a consequence of our love for him, but it is also a command from Allah. The Qur'an equates the following of the Prophet's Sunnah with our obedience to Allah's commands. This is why the Qur'an and the Sunnah are considered as two non-variable sources of *Shari'ah*. The Sunnah is not secondary in nature, rather it is the second source of law.

The *ayah, "[O Messenger, tell the people:] 'If you indeed love Allah, follow me, and Allah will love you and will forgive you your sins. Allah is All-Forgiving, All-Compassionate*'" (Al 'Imran 3: 31) conveys three very clear commands.

First, all people—not only Muslims—who claim to love God (with whatever name they address Him by) are told that the Final Messenger ﷺ is not particular to the Muslims, rather, anyone who loves his/her God is expected to follow the Prophet's exemplary conduct and behaviour.

Second, it is a request of faith that no discrimination is made between a Qur'anic command and a verified Sunnah or hadith of the Prophet ﷺ. If they really love Allah, they must follow the Prophet ﷺ.

Third, *Shari'ah* is not confined to the Qur'an but includes the Prophetic Sunnah as well. It is the Qur'an, and not the Prophet ﷺ, which, in explicit terms, says: "*He who obeys the Messenger thereby obeys Allah.*" (al-Nisa' 4: 80) Similarly, if a believer disregards the Prophetic Sunnah, it is no different than violating Allah's commands in the Qur'an: "*Say [O Prophet]: 'Obey Allah and obey the Messenger.' But if they turn away from this, then know that Allah does not love the disbelievers.*" (Al 'Imran 3: 32)

In the earlier *ayah*, emulating the Prophet's ways was linked to the love of Allah, the believers were told that love of Allah means not only verbal praise, but also strict adherence to what is prescribed in the *Shari'ah*. In this *ayah*, the conversation is summed up with a clear directive that if human beings hoped to save themselves in the life Hereafter, then the only path for them is to obey Allah, obey His Messenger ﷺ, and to deliver their responsibilities with honesty and truthfulness.

The underlying theme in the narrative remains *tawhid*. It is *tawhid* which demands unconditional obedience to Allah and His Messenger ﷺ.

It is due to *tawhid* that love and obedience cannot be shared with more than One Beloved.

Tawhid refers to observing the Unity of Allah, not only in His person, but also in His attributes. Therefore, no one can be considered eternally living (*al-Hayy*), perfectly knowledgeable (*al-'Alim*) and infinitely powerful (*al-Qawiyy, al-Qadir*) but Allah. Consequently, the claim which some esoteric groups make about people being alive after their physical death is set aside by the Qur'an. It implies that Maryam and 'Isa in themselves had no divinity, though the former has been elevated above all women of the world and the latter is given a special status in and by the Qur'an: "*Then came the time when the angels said: 'O Mary! Surely, Allah has chosen you, and has made you pure, and has exalted you above all the women in the world.'*" (Al 'Imran 3: 42) She is exalted above all women in the world but not made a partner in divinity.

"*Whenever Zachariah visited her in the sanctuary, he found her provided with rizq.*" (Al 'Imran 3: 37) This *ayah* has been interpreted in two ways: an obvious meaning for the word *rizq*, or provision, here is eatables, such as fruit or cooked food. The other interpretation alludes to Maryam's conversations which showed depth in terms of knowledge, maturity and wisdom beyond her age. When asked about where she got this *hikmah* from, her answer was that she was fed this wisdom, i.e., that she received it, from her Lord. This persuaded Zakariyyah to make *du'a'* to Allah, beseeching Him to bless him with a child with a character as noble as Maryam's. But he also knew that he was already too old and that his wife was barren. It was hoping against all odds, yet he made *du'a'* as a true believer.

Allah responded to the prayer of Zakariyyah because nothing is impossible with Him. He only says, "Be" (*Kun*) and it is there. Zakariyyah was given the good news of a baby boy who will be named Yahya [John], a name which was not given to any child before him. The birth of Yahya, in such a situation itself was a miracle. All miracles are performed by the One Who is above every law, the Real Lawmaker, the Creator Who controls everything. Therefore, no miracle can be attributed to any human being.

From her mother's side, Maryam was from the family of Harūn [Aron] the family of priests. This is why when Maryam's mother conceived, she vowed to dedicate her newborn as a devotee in the temple. But when the child that was born was a baby girl, she wondered how she could fulfill her wish, as it was not customary to have a girl as a devotee in the sanctuary. It was an unusual situation. Moreover, a girl could not be accepted in the sanctuary without a guardian. Therefore, a draw was made and one of the priests in the sanctuary, Zakariyyah, was appointed as her guardian. It so happened that Zakariyyah was also a close relative of Maryam; he was her maternal uncle.

The episode continues and the Qur'an provides details which were not given by the earlier Scriptures. Maryam was informed through an angel that she was going to conceive a baby boy who would be a Prophet. She responded with astonishment, questioning as to how that would be possible when no man had touched her. The angel told her that this was Allah's command and so it shall be.

In all three cases—the birth of Yahya when Zakariyyah's wife was barren; the birth of 'Isa when Maryam was a virgin; and the talking of 'Isa from the cradle and later, his performing several other miracles—proves the supremacy of the Power and Command of Allah.

In other words, these extraordinary events provide undeniable evidence of the transcendence of Allah's Command and Power, and His Uniqueness, Sovereignty, and Unity. These miracles were misinterpreted by the followers of 'Isa who thought that he was divine in nature and it was he who performed these miracles. The Qur'an asserts that these miracles were, in actuality, caused by the Command of Allah. The word *kun* (meaning, "Be") is the Word pronounced by Allah which allowed Maryam to conceive without any human touching her.

When the Qur'an refers to 'Isa as "the *kalimah* of Allah", it simply means that he himself is evidence or *kalimah* of how a command can cause things without following a natural course. The truth is all miracles take place at the Command "*kun*" of Allah. No one except Him can cause a miracle. If, as they claim, miracles were caused by 'Isa due to his divine powers, it will imply that there is a power-sharing dynamic between Allah and him, which is a logical contradiction and contrary to the original teaching of 'Isa in relation to the Unity and Transcendence of the Creator God. On the other hand, those who denied his Prophethood called these miracles an act of magic and sorcery.

Against this backdrop, let us read the Qur'anic narrative: *"Truly, Allah chose Adam, and Noah, the descendants of Abraham, and of 'Imran above all mankind (for His Messengership) – a people alike and the seed of one another. Allah is All-Hearing, All-Knowing. (He also heard) when 'Imran's woman said: 'O Lord! Indeed, I dedicate what is in my womb to Your exclusive service. So accept it from me. Surely, You alone are All-Hearing, All-Knowing.' But when she delivered a female child, she said: 'O Lord! I have given birth to a female—and Allah knew full well what she had given birth to—and the male is not the same as the female. I have named her Mary and commit her offspring to You for protection from Satan, the accursed.'*

Thereupon, her Lord graciously accepted Mary and vouchsafed to her a goodly growth, placing her in the care of Zachariah.

Whenever Zachariah visited her in the sanctuary, he found her supplied with provisions [rizq]. He asked her: 'O Mary! How did this come to you?' She said: 'It is from Allah. Allah provides sustenance to whom He wills beyond all reckoning.' Then and there, Zachariah prayed to his Lord: 'My Lord! Grant me from Yourself—out of Your Grace and gift—a goodly offspring. Indeed, You alone are the Hearer of all prayers.'

As he stood praying in the sanctuary the angels called out to him: 'Allah gives you good tidings of John (Yahya), who shall confirm a command of Allah, shall be outstanding among people, utterly chaste, and a Prophet from among the righteous.' Zachariah exclaimed: 'My Lord! How shall I have a son when old age has overtaken me, and my wife is barren?' He said: 'Thus shall it be. Allah does what He wills.' Zachariah said: 'My Lord! Appoint a Sign for me.' He said: 'The Sign for you shall be that you shall not [be able to] speak to people for three days except by gestures. Remember your Lord and extol His Glory by night and day.'" (Al 'Imran 3: 33–41)

"*[And remember] when the angels said: 'O Mary! Surely, Allah has chosen you, and made you pure, and exalted you above all women in the world. O Mary! Remain devout to your Lord, prostrate yourself in worship and bow down with those who bow down [before Him].' (O Muhammad) that We reveal to you this account from a realm which lies beyond the reach of your perception for you were not with them when they disputed about it.*" (Al 'Imran 3: 42–44)

"*And when the angels said: 'O Mary! Allah gives you the glad tidings of a Command from Him: his name shall be Messiah, Jesus, the son of Mary. He shall be highly honoured in this world and in the Hereafter and shall be one of those near-stationed [to Allah]. And he shall speak to people in the cradle and adulthood and shall indeed be among the righteous.' She said: 'My Lord! How shall I have a son when no man has ever touched me?' [An angel] answered:*

'Thus shall it be. Allah creates whatever He wills. When He decides something, He merely says, "Be!" and it is. And He will teach him the Book, the wisdom, the Torah, and the Gospel.'" (Al 'Imran 3: 45–48)

The train of Prophets sent to Bani Isra'il was an indication of Allah's *rahmah* and *'adl* to remind them time and again about the covenant they made with their Lord, to worship none but Him and live a life of balance, moderation and obedience to Him. But the several-thousand-year long history of the Bani Isra'il, parts of which are mirrored in the Qur'an, indicates their ungratefulness to their *Rabb*. The coming of 'Isa [Jesus], flanked by Yahya [John] was but one such reminder and blessing.

The story of the birth of 'Isa, narrated briefly in the above *ayat*, in itself provides evidence of his being a true Messenger of Allah. In a sense, he was the second Adam. The first one was born without any biological parents, was made from dust and was fully fashioned and made alive by the command of Allah's "*kun*". In the case of 'Isa, no man touched Maryam, yet Allah's command "be" or "*kun*" caused the biological process to start; and the priests of Bani Isra'il as well as the common men, all witnessed in daylight, 'Isa, who from his cradle declared that he was the Messiah, son of Mary; was given guidance from Allah; and was Allah's messenger sent to Bani Isra'il from among themselves.

His mother's family background was well-known to the people, and all the priests in the temple respected her for her piety, wisdom and devotion. Maryam's maternal uncle was chief priest, and from her mother's side, she was a granddaughter of Harūn [Aaron], the brother of Musa [Moses]. The miraculous birth of 'Isa was later misinterpreted by his followers as a sign of his divinity, though it was evident that his birth was due to a command of Allah Who has no partner in His Divinity.

Since Bani Isra'il had a history of behaving unfairly with their Prophets, and of incessantly demanding them to perform miracles to prove their Prophethood, 'Isa informed them that Allah had gifted him with many miracles, like giving life to a bird that was made out of clay by pronouncing the name of Allah over it; healing a leper and a blind person; and even making a dead person come back to life—all with the permission of Allah—as visible proof of his Prophethood.

*"And he will be a Messenger to the Children of Israel." (And when he came to them he said): "I have come to you with a Sign from your Lord. I will make for you from clay the likeness of a bird and then I will breathe into it and by the leave of Allah it will become a bird. I will also heal the blind and the leper, and by the leave of Allah I will bring the dead to life. I will also inform you of what things you eat and what you treasure up in your houses. Surely this is a Sign for you if you are true believers." (*Al 'Imran *3: 49)*

But all of this evidence did not convince them. They denied accepting him as Allah's Messenger and refuted his message. The *da'wah* he gave was to take only Allah as their Lord who sent him with those undeniable miracles. He never once instructed them to take him as God or the son of God because of those miracles he came with. He never attributed the miracles to his own ability; rather he kept reiterating that they were all granted to him and permitted by none other than the One true God, Allah.

Prophet 'Isa called himself only an *'abd*, a servant, of Allah who was sent to Bani Isra'il to remind them about the faith of their forefathers—specifically, the faith of Ibrahim, Musa, Dawud, Sulayman, and others—which stated that Ultimate Supremacy, Authority, Uniqueness and Unity, all, belongs to Allah alone. Therefore, He alone should be served.

Here, after referring briefly to the elevated status of Maryam as being above all the women of the world, the Qur'an mentions the virgin birth of 'Isa as evidence of his Prophethood and as an important chapter in the history of Bani Isra'il. These *ayat* are addressed to both the Bani Isra'il (specifically referring to the Jews) and the Nasara (the Christians) in order to remind them of their unfair attitude and behaviour towards 'Isa and his followers, who were persecuted for no other crime but declaring their faith in the One and Only Allah, which was no different than the faith of Musa and other Prophets.

These *ayat* also provided food for thought to the Christian delegation from Najran who visited Madinah to have a dialogue with the Prophet ﷺ. These *ayat* told them about the Muslims' belief in the truthfulness of the Prophethood of 'Isa, his miraculous birth, and the elevated and respectful status of Maryam, which in turn, provided a common ground for an interfaith dialogue. It also provided an opportunity to make them realize the irrationality of their considering 'Isa as divine and the son of God, while he himself never claimed any divinity. He always preached *tawhid* and obedience to Allah alone who is neither begotten nor begets. Even so, besides a handful of followers (the *hawari* or *ansar*, the helpers), a majority of the Bani Isra'il remained adamant unbelievers and opposed the Prophethood of 'Isa.

Prophet 'Isa's Clear Message

It is important to carefully study the words used by 'Isa while inviting Bani Isra'il to Allah's obedience: "*I have come to confirm the truth of whatever there still remains of the Torah and to make lawful some of the things which had been forbidden for you. I have come to you with a Sign from your Lord; so have fear of Allah and obey me. Surely, Allah is my Lord and your Lord; so serve Him alone. This is the Straight Way.*" (Al 'Imran 3: 50-51)

Every single word of 'Isa conveys volumes of meaning. First, he clearly declares that he has not come with a new faith but to reconfirm, "Whatever there still remains of the Torah", tells Bani Isra'il that they did not protect or preserve their Lord's commandments in full, and only a part of the Torah remains with them, the rest of it lost due to their irresponsibility.

Second, he is not talking about what has been lost by them, but he wants to reaffirm what remained in the Torah with them; therefore, they have no justification in opposing him.

Third, he has come with clear signs from Allah because Bani Isra'il always demanded a display of miracles from their Prophets in order to prove that they were genuine Prophets of Allah. Clearly, 'Isa's birth itself was enough evidence for his being Allah's Messenger, and for his truthfulness.

Fourth, the message he conveys to them is not to regard him as divine or as sharing in Allah's Divinity, but to obey and follow their Lord alone and shun all other obedience and deviant, evil ways (*tawaghit*). He further says that he has come to make certain things permissible for them which they, without any evidence, had made forbidden (*haram*) upon themselves. In other words, the scholars of Bani Isra'il had taken liberty in changing the Scripture according to their own whims and desires. 'Isa says that he has come to reverse all that.

These *ayat* illustrate the unity in *da'wah* of not only 'Isa with what the Prophet ﷺ offered to the Jews and Christians, but also unity with the message conveyed by all Messengers of Allah, including Ibrahim, Musa and others.

Having made clear that his task is to remind them about worshipping Allah, and no other deity, he sums up his message: "*Surely Allah is my Lord and your Lord so serve Him alone. This is the Straight way.*" (Al 'Imran 3: 51) Despite knowing well that Prophet 'Isa was the truthful Messenger of Allah, very few Israelites responded favourably to him: "*And when Jesus perceived their leaning towards unbelief, he asked: 'Who will be my helpers in the way of Allah?' The disciples said: We are the helpers of Allah, we believe in Allah and be our witness that we have submitted ourselves exclusively to Allah. Our Lord! We believe in the commandments You have revealed and we obey the Messenger, make us then, one of those who bear witness [to the Truth].*" (Al 'Imran 3:52-53)

Keeping these *ayat* in mind, we can see for ourselves great similarities in how the Qur'an talks about the mission of the Final Messenger ﷺ: "*Those who follow the unlettered [ummi] Prophet whom they find mentioned in the Torah and Gospel that they have. He enjoins upon them what is good and forbids them what is evil. He makes the clean things lawful to them and prohibits all corrupt things, and removes from them their burdens and the shackles that were upon them. So those who believe in him and follow the Light (the Qur'an) which has been sent down with him, it is they who shall prosper.*" (al-A'raf 7: 157)

With this brief resume of Maryam and 'Isa, his unique birth and his undeniable miracles, the Qur'an underscores the unjust behaviour of the Bani Isra'il towards him. Instead of following the Truth he brought to them, they behaved with the same arrogance as they observed towards the earlier Messengers of Allah: "*Then they schemed [against the Messiah] and Allah countered their schemes by schemes of His own. Allah is the best of schemers (and it was part of His scheme). When Allah said: 'O Jesus! I will recall you, and raise you up to Me, and will purify you [of the company] of those who disbelieve, and will set your followers above the unbelievers till the Day of Resurrection. Then to Me shall all of you return, and I shall judge between you regarding whatever you differed among yourselves. As for those who disbelieved, I shall inflict a terrible chastisement on them in this world and in the Hereafter, and they shall find none to help them.*

But those who believe and do righteous deeds, they will be rewarded in full. Allah does not love the unjust. What We recite to you consists of signs and wise admonition.'" (Al 'Imran 3: 54–58)

The Qur'an dispels attributing any divine characteristics to 'Isa: "*Surely in the sight of Allah, the similitude of the creation of Jesus is as the creation of Adam. He created him out of dust and then said, 'Be!' and he was. This is the truth from your Lord, be not then among those who doubt.*" (Al 'Imran 3: 58-59) The Qur'anic argument is simple: If a miraculous birth is sufficient proof to make Jesus the son of God or God, then the birth of Adam without a father *and* mother should make Adam super-divine!

The Qur'anic Invitation for a Dialogue

If such sound arguments do not convince the People of the Book, the Qur'an invites them for a *mubahalah,* (a trial through power), i.e., they may bring with them their family members and take an oath asking Allah to adjudicate the matter between the believers and the People of the Book who dispute with the Prophet ﷺ. In case they withdraw and hesitate in taking an oath, this shall prove the invalidity of their position. The Christian delegation preferred not to come forward for the *mubahalah.*

"*This is the truth from your Lord; be not then among those who doubt. Tell whoever disputes with you on this matter after true knowledge has come to you: 'Come let us summon our sons and your son's, and our women and your women, and ourselves and yourselves, and then let us pray together and invoke the curse of Allah on those who lie.' This is the true story. There is no god but Allah, and assuredly Allah is All-Mighty All-Wise. And if they turn their backs, truly Allah knows those who cause mischief.*" (Al 'Imran 3: 60-63)

Having said that, the Qur'an extends an open invitation for an engagement with the people of the Book through dialogue: "*Say: 'People of the Book! Come to a word common between us and you, that we shall serve none but Allah and shall associate none with Him [in His Divinity] and that some of us will not take others as lords other than Allah.' And if they turn away [from accepting this call], then say: 'Bear witness that we are the ones who have submitted ourselves [exclusively to Allah].'*" (Al 'Imran 3: 64)

The Qur'an invites both the Bani Isra'il and the followers of 'Isa, who also took Ibrahim as their patriarch, to understand that Ibrahim was a true believer in *tawhid* and that he rejected all forms of associationism (*shirk*). Therefore, those who assign divinity to 'Isa, or 'Uzayr (in case of the Jews), make a deviation from the faith of Ibrahim, while Islam is no more and no less than a call towards the *din* of Ibrahim: "*Say: 'As for me, my Lord has guided me to the Straight Way, a right din, the way of Abraham, the upright, who was not of the polytheists.' Say: 'Surely my prayer, my worship, my living and my dying are only for Allah, the Lord of the whole universe. He has no associate. Thus, have I been bidden, and I am the foremost of those who submit (muslimin) themselves [to Allah].'"* (al-An'am 6: 161–163)

The Qur'an also invites the People of the Book to refer to their own Scriptures, the Old Testament and the New Testament which recognize Ibrahim as their patriarch. The Bani Isra'il call themselves Jews while the followers of 'Isa call themselves Christians. The Qur'an asks them what was the faith of Ibrahim? Did he ever call himself an ethnic Jew? Or a Christian? Secondly, if it is necessary for one to be from the seed of Dawud to be successful or to believe in 'Isa's crucifixion for redemption, then what shall be the status of Ibrahim himself? He was neither a Jew nor a Christian. Is it not more logical and rational for both the Jews and the Christians to follow the *din* of their forefather Ibrahim who was followed in word and spirit by Ishaq, Ya'qub, Sulayman, Dawud, Musa, Isma'il and Muhammad ﷺ.

The Qur'an asks in a simple, non-theological manner: "*O People of the Book, why do you dispute with us about Abraham even though the Torah and the Gospel were not revealed until after his time? Do you not understand? Behold! You are those who have severely disputed concerning matters of which you have knowledge; why are you now disputing concerning matters that you know nothing about? Allah knows it whereas you do not know.*" (Al 'Imran 3: 65–66)

The Qur'an further settles the controversy created by the Jewish and Christian theologies:

"*Abraham was neither a Jew nor a Christian; he was a Muslim, wholly devoted to God. And he was not amongst the polytheists [those who associate others with Allah in His Divinity]. Surely, the people who have the best claim to affiliation with Abraham are those who followed him [in the past], and [presently] this Prophet and those who believe in him. Allah is the guardian of those who truly believe.*" (Al 'Imran 3: 67–68)

POINT TO PONDER

Anyone who uses common sense can see the simple, rational, unbiased and dialogical approach of the Qur'an towards the People of the Book (the Jews and Christians in particular) to invite them to think at a conceptual and historical level.

Conceptually, the message of Ibrahim was uncompromising *tawhid*, Oneness and Uniqueness of Allah. Historically, the original teaching in the Jewish and Christian Scripture was that of *tawhid* and never of *shirk* or associationism. Therefore, the Qur'an offers a common ground for dialogue with regards to the belief in the One and Only Creator, Allah, as well as the belief in the Final Judgement in the *Akhirah*. Those who believe in these two realities are invited to cooperate in matters of virtue, goodness and fairness, and join the believers in fighting against evil, obscenity, injustice and lawlessness in society.

The Qur'an refers to the psyche of the People of the Book—that even when they have no iota of doubt about the truthfulness of the Prophet ﷺ and about the Divine nature of the Qur'an, they still hesitate to give up the tradition of their forefathers. Instead of embracing the Truth, they wanted to confuse the believers and if possible, even persuade them to revert to the ways of ignorance, "*A party of the People of the Book would preferably lead you astray, whereas in truth they lead none astray except themselves, yet they do not realize it. O People of the Book! Why do you reject the signs of Allah even though you yourself witness them? O People of the Book! Why do you confound the Truth with falsehood, and why do you conceal the Truth knowingly? A party of the People of the Book said [to one another]: 'Believe in the morning what has been revealed to those who believe, and then deny it in the evening that they may retract (from their faith).*'" (Al 'Imran 3: 69–72)

This dualism of the People of the Book is not hidden from Allah. While exposing their non-seriousness, the Qur'an follows a soft *da'wah* approach: *"They also say among themselves. 'Do not follow anyone except him who follows your faith.' Say: 'Surely true guidance is Allah's. It is His favour that anyone should be given the like of what you have been given in the past and that others should have been given firm evidence to proffer against you before your Lord'. Say 'Surely bounty is in the hands of Allah; He gives it to whom He wills. Allah is All-Embracing, All-Knowing. He singles out for His Mercy whomever He wills. Allah is All-Embracing, All-Knowing.'"* (Al 'Imran 3: 73–74)

In other words, those who refuse to accept Allah's favour, or His bounty in the form of guidance sent as the Qur'an, and the role model of the Prophet ﷺ, they themselves are responsible for their misfortune.

But not all of Bani Isra'il were the same. There were exceptions: "*There are some among the People of the Book who will restore you even if you were to entrust a treasure of gold, and among them are also others, who, were you to entrust one gold piece, will not restore it unless you stand over them. That is because they say: 'We will not be taken to task for whatever we may do to non-Jews [ummiyyin].' Thus, they falsely fix a lie upon Allah, and do so wittingly. But Allah loves only those who fulfill their covenant and fear Allah. Truly, Allah loves the God-fearing [muttaqin]. There shall be no share in the life to come for those who sell away the covenant of Allah and their oaths for a trivial gain. On the Day of Resurrection, Allah will neither address them nor look at them, nor will He purify them. A grievous chastisement awaits them.*" (Al 'Imran 3: 75–77)

Invitation to Return to the Original Faith

While providing solid evidence on the deviance of the Bani Isra'il from the clear directions of their Scripture, the Qur'an follows a balanced and objective approach. It does not blame all Bani Isra'il for the wrongs of a few of them.

At the same time, it exposes various tactics and strategies that were used by them to hide their hate for Islam and the final Prophet ﷺ. For instance, some of the mischievous persons in the Bani Isra'il pronounced words in a way as if they were divine revelation while they were nothing but their own creation. Referring to this practice, the Qur'an raises a simple question about the content of their narrative, namely, how is it possible that a revelation they attribute to Allah can contain a command to worship and obey someone other than Allah? Could Ibrahim, Musa or 'Isa, as Messengers of Allah ever ask their followers to worship anyone other than Allah or ask their followers to believe in their own divinity and thus worship them?

"*There is a party among them who twist their tongues while reciting the Book to make you think that it is part of the Book, when in fact it is not. They say, 'It is from Allah', when in fact it is not from Allah. They falsely fix a lie upon Allah and do so wittingly.*

It does not befit a man that Allah should grant him His Book and sound judgement and prophethood and thereafter he should say to the people: 'Become servants to me apart from Allah.' He would rather say: 'Become dedicated men of Allah, in accord with the dictates of the Book you have been teaching and studying.' He will never enjoin you to take the angels or Prophets for your lords. Will he enjoin upon you unbelief when you have submitted yourselves to Allah?" (Al 'Imran 3: 78–80)

The Qur'an reminds Bani Isra'il about their wrong attitude toward their Prophets, i.e., their attribution of divine characteristics to them. At the same time, it also reminds them about a pledge they had made as a community to recognize and follow all Messengers sent to them, including the Final Messenger ﷺ of Allah: "*Surely, Allah took a covenant with the Children of Israel and We raised up from them twelve of their leaders, and Allah said: 'Behold! I am with you if you establish prayer, pay zakah, believe in My Prophets, help them, and lend Allah a goodly loan; I will certainly efface from you, your evil deeds and will surely cause you to enter the Gardens beneath which rivers flow.'*" (al-Ma'idah 5: 12)

Later, in *Surah al-A'raf*, specific reference is made to the Final Messenger ﷺ in their Scripture, with instructions to follow him: "*[Today the Mercy is for] those who follow the unlettered [ummi] Prophet, whom they find mentioned in the Torah and the Gospel that they have. He enjoins upon them what is good and forbids them what is evil. He makes the clean things lawful [halal] to them and prohibits all corrupt things [khaba'ith], and removes from them their burden and the shackles that were upon them. So those who believe in him and assist him and succour him and follow the Light which has been sent down with him, it is they who shall prosper.*" (al-A'raf 7: 157)

The message conveyed is three-fold. First and foremost, all Messengers of Allah called human beings to obey only Allah, to whom they all submit with all possible devotions. Second, since all Messengers of Allah brought one and the same common message of obedience to the Creator, the Sustainer, the Most Powerful, Kind and Loving Allah, consequently, belief in the truthfulness of all Messengers of Allah becomes an article of faith. Third, the People of the Book were clearly informed in their own Scripture about the coming of the Final Messenger ﷺ to be, not in the progeny of Ishaq, but in the lineage of Isma'il. The Bani Isra'il, therefore, had no excuse in insisting that they will follow only Prophets who belonged to the lineages of Ishaq and Dawud. In other words, Islam's *da'wah* to the People of the Book was no different than what their own Scriptures originally asked them to follow. Those who reject the Qur'anic message actually deviate from their own Scripture and from the instructions contained in the uncorrupted, original form of that Scripture. How could they claim to be a "chosen people" destined to go to Paradise while they blatantly break the covenant of obedience they made with their Lord?

This dispassionate, logical, nonpartisan and sympathetic approach of the Qur'an is reflected from cover to cover when it addresses the Bani Isra'il. The Most Compassionate knows well their breaking of the covenant of obedience which they made with their Lord. The same message is conveyed in other places in the Qur'an, for example: "*Say [O Prophet]: 'All Praise be to Allah and peace be on those of His servants whom He has chosen.' [Ask the disbelievers:] 'Who is better: Allah or whatever [false gods] they associate [with Him as His partners]? Who is it that has created the heavens and the earth, and sent down for you water from the sky, and then We caused to grow therewith orchards full of beauty whose trees you could never cause to grow. Is there any god associated with Allah?' Nay! they are a people who are veering away from the right path."* (al-Naml 27: 59–60)

The Common Faith of the Messengers

The fact of the matter is the uncompromising Unity of Allah or *tawhid* alone has been the basic teaching of all the Messengers.

It is an obvious deviation from their Divine guidance to consider religious leaders, rabbis or even the Prophets as their protectors and saviours. The only Savior and Protector is Allah, the *Rabb* of Ibrahim, Ishaq, Isma'il and of all the Messengers of Bani Isra'il.

The essence of the covenant the Bani Isra'il made with their Lord was to follow unadulterated, pure *tawhid* in all aspects of life: "*Recall when Allah took a covenant from the Prophets: 'This is the Book and the Wisdom which I have granted you. But should a Prophet come to you confirming what you already possess, you shall believe in him and shall help him.' So saying, Allah asked: 'Do you agree and accept to take up the burden of the covenant?' They answered: 'We agree.' He said: 'Then bear witness, and I will be with you among the witnesses.' Then whosoever shall turn away from this covenant, they are the transgressors.*" (Al 'Imran 3: 81–82)

Whenever Musa received instructions in the form of *wahi,* he would call his followers to the prayer camp, where the relics were kept in a sacred box or case (*tabut*), and he would not only communicate to them Divine instructions but also take from them an oath to implement them. This is why the Qur'an often reminds the Bani Isra'il about the pledges and covenants they made with their Lord in the presence of Musa.

After referring to the covenant the Bani Isra'il made—that they will follow and support Prophets sent by Allah, including the Final Messenger ﷺ or the Messenger sent to an *ummi* people—the Qur'an questions the reason for Bani Isra'il's hesitation in welcoming the Islamic message: "*Do they now seek a religion [din] other than that prescribed by Allah, and this despite all that is in the heavens and the earth is in submission to Him—willingly or unwillingly—and to Him all shall return? Say: 'We believe in Allah and what was revealed to us and what was revealed to Abraham, Ishmael, Isaac, Jacob and to his descendants; and the teachings of which Allah gave to Moses, Jesus and other Prophets. We make no distinction between any of them and to Him do we submit.*'" (Al 'Imran 3: 83–84)

The Original Faith of Mankind

The Qur'an provides undeniable evidence from the Scriptures of the Bani Isra'il on their original faith—obedience to Allah, the Creator Lord of all animate and inanimate things. It also refers to their own history of acting against their Scripture, of inserting into their Scripture their own ideas and claiming them as inspired by their God. While confirming whatever remained unpolluted in their Scripture, the Qur'an invites them to follow the fully protected message of the Qur'an, which is sent by the same Authority as the final guidance for the people of the world. At this point, the Qur'an announces that this final Scripture, the Qur'an, substitutes all earlier Scriptures due to its comprehensiveness, its complete preservation and its universal applicability in diverse human situations. The Qur'anic view is that ultimate Truth must be one and not many. Since the Qur'an is historically the only fully protected Speech of Allah, there is no justification for following any man-made ideology or faith.

"And whoever seeks a way other than this way of submission – Islam – will find that it will not be accepted from him and he will be among the losers in the Life to Come. How can Allah guide a people who once believed, and after they had received Clear Signs and affirmed that the Messenger was a true one, they lapsed into disbelief? Allah does not guide the wrongdoers. The recompense for their wrongdoings is that the curse of Allah, and of the angels, and of all of men shall be upon them. Thus, shall they abide. Neither shall their chastisement be lightened nor shall they be granted any respite. But for those who repent and mend their ways, Allah is indeed Most Forgiving, Most Compassionate. Indeed, those who disbelieve after having believed and then hardened in their disbelief, their [pretense to] repentance will never be accepted. Such have utterly gone astray. Truly those who embraced unbelief and died as disbelievers, not even the whole earth full of gold will be accepted from them as ransom. For such there is a painful chastisement, and none shall come to their help." (Al 'Imran 3: 85–91)

Here, the Qur'an makes it clear for us that since the Bani Isra'il repeatedly violated their pledge of following their Scripture and kept adding and changing in what was revealed to them, it was necessary to send down an authentic revelation, which may also refer to earlier teachings. Allah does not want human beings to be left without guidance, *hidayah,* because He loves them. He wants them to make their way to *Jannah* and does not want them to suffer due to misguidance in this world and face chastisement in the life Hereafter. This Compassion and Kindness is specific to Allah. He forgives all those who return to Him sincerely and mend their ways. He is so Compassionate that if a wrongdoer takes one step towards Him, He takes ten steps towards them.

It also reconfirms the fact that all Messengers of Allah were sent to remind people about the one and only Truth, i.e., to obey none but Allah and become Muslim—one who submits to and consciously serves Allah. This is why it is stated that no faith other than Islam shall be accepted as the way of life from any community of the people.

In the *ayah* 83 of *Al' Imran*, a query was made: *"Do they now seek a religion [din] other than that prescribed by Allah, knowing that all that is in the heavens and the earth is in submission to Him—willingly or unwillingly...?"* which makes it clear that every object in the universe, small or big, animate or inanimate is following the way prescribed for it by the Creator, Allah. Therefore, it is only logical and natural for human beings as well to obey the directions of their Creator. If they act otherwise, it will be a deviation from their *fitrah*, their natural disposition and innate constitution. The difference, however, remains that the mountains, rivers, birds and fish have no choice but to follow the natural course prescribed for them, whereas human beings are gifted with the freedom of will. Therefore, it is up to them to follow *fitrah*, the path to success and felicity or the path to failure and torment.

At least three lessons can be drawn from the above Qur'anic statement. First, the Qur'an, due to its universality and authenticity, is distinct from the earlier Scriptures that were sent to specific people at given times for their guidance. Second, since Islam includes the original teachings of all earlier Messengers of Allah—who called towards servitude to Allah and the rejection of all other obedience—and since nothing has been lost, changed, added or missed in the Qur'an, allowing it to remain fully preserved in its original form—both in recorded text and within the memory of millions of believers, with no variation between them—reason demands us to follow it without any hesitation. Third, since not only the Book remains intact, but also because its embodiment in the perfect model, behaviour and conduct of the Prophet ﷺ is fully preserved, there remains no need for any Messenger or Prophet to come after him. Any claim to be a Prophet (*nabi*) or Messenger (*rasul*) made by anyone after the Prophethood of Muhammad ﷺ shall be false and considered an act of *kufr* (as in the case of Qadiyani or Ahamadis).

The *ayah* also implies that the Bani Isra'il and the Christians should be grateful to Allah for reviving the original teachings of their Messengers through the authentic narrations of the Qur'an. In fact, the Qur'an offers hope to all those who followed the earlier revelations, "*But for those who repent and mend their ways, Allah is Most Forgiving, Most Compassionate.*" (Al 'Imran 3: 89)

If a wrong is committed unintentionally or due to forgetfulness, Allah is extremely Kind, Forgiving and Compassionate towards His servants. But if a people repeatedly and arrogantly persist in violating His commands, it is a demand of *'adl* or fairness to reprimand them, "*Truly those who embraced unbelief and died as disbelievers, not even the whole earth full of gold will be accepted from them as ransom. For such there is a painful chastisement, and none shall come to their help.*" (Al 'Imran 3: 91) Greed and love of wealth, power, and authority is a common human weakness; the Bani Isra'il were no exception to it. The Qur'an refers to this human phenomenon in the context of the Day of Judgement—that when defaulters shall see with their own eyes what kind of punishment is awaiting them, they would yearn to sacrifice all the gold and wealth they had once loved in order to save themselves from the torment. But no recompense will be accepted at that time.

The general principle underscored by the Qur'an at this point is that a believer should try to attain true God-consciousness (*taqwa*) and virtue (*birr*) in this worldly life, before the Day of Judgement arrives, in order to have success (*falah* and *sa'adah*) in the life Hereafter. A believer should be prepared to sacrifice and offer whatever he/she can afford, in the way of Allah, just to seek His pleasure. *Taqwa* of a person can be easily measured by looking into a variety of things, such as how regularly a person performs voluntary prayers over and above the obligatory prayers; how frequently he/she gives *sadaqah* along with the mandatory payment of zakah, and takes care of those who are in debt, difficulties and so on.

When we compare major world religions, we find several common themes, such as the existence of a Divine Being, the Final Judgement of man, a Scripture, and the need for a hero or role model. Among the religions which believe in Divine revelation, Islam, in a sense, is the youngest and at the same time, the oldest faith as a way of life. The Qur'an informs us that the faith of Prophet Nuh, Ibrahim, Isma'il, Ishaq, Musa and 'Isa was none other than Islam—the total acceptance of Allah as the Creator Lord and to serve Him alone. In that context, Islam is not new but the universal faith of all Messengers of Allah.

The Qur'an also invites human beings to look critically into the unique synergy and regularity in the universe, which cannot be a random phenomenon. It is designed by none other than Allah. The followers of the Old and the New Testaments in particular, and others in general, are reminded by the Qur'an to follow the original teaching of their own Scriptures and denounce all man-made gods. It keeps reminding them that all Messengers of Bani Isra'il, including 'Isa asked people to submit to the One and Only Lord of the universe. Their *da'wah* was none other than *tawhid*. Therefore, if someone wants to achieve success in the life Hereafter, one should excel in ethical and moral conduct. Sacrificing resources such as wealth is one desirable activity. The Qur'an motivates believers to spend in the way of Allah: "*You shall not attain righteousness until you spend for the sake of Allah out of what you love. Allah knows whatever you spend.*" (Al 'Imran 3: 92)

The Path of Ibrahim

Just as *tawhid* is the core teaching of Islam, the Qur'an reminds us that it was also the basic message of Ibrahim. He went through a series of tests and trials only for upholding *tawhid*. Therefore, if the People of the Book truly believe in the path of Ibrahim, they should not hesitate in embracing Islam. The Qur'an further elaborates that Islamic teachings are no different than the practice of Ibrahim. Whatever was allowed in his Divine Law (*Shari'ah*) is also allowed in the Islamic *Shari'ah*.

It was a common practice among the Bani Isra'il that camel meat and camel milk was avoided. Due to this Jewish practice, even today, non-dairy coffee creamer is produced and marketed in the US and Europe. The Qur'an corrects this practice and mentions that the patriarch, Ibrahim had in fact allowed and used the milk and meat of camels. Though Ya'qub [Jacob] avoided use of camel meat due to his personal dislike, it was never prohibited in the Torah. The Prophet ﷺ, therefore, following the path of Ibrahim, used both the meat and milk of camel which makes it a Sunnah of both Ibrahim and the final Prophet ﷺ.

One universal principle the Qur'an prescribes is: that which is pure, clean, and healthy (*tayyib*) by nature is permissible, and all that which is unclean (*khabith*) by nature is prohibited. Wealth acquired by ethical means is a blessing or *fadl*, while wealth acquired from unethical means is unclean and cannot be purified by giving away a part of it in charity. The same principle applies for food. Liquor and intoxicants, by nature, are unclean whether in small quantity or large. The Qur'an questions this practice of the Jewish community of prohibiting eating meat and milk together, and asks Jewish scholars to produce evidence from their Scripture regarding the same: "*All food [that is lawful in Islamic Shari'ah] was lawful to the Children of Israel, except what Israel made unlawful to themselves before the revelation of Torah. Tell them [O Prophet]: 'Bring the Torah and read it, if you are truthful.' Those who forge lies against Allah are the wrongdoers. Say [O Prophet]: Allah has declared the truth. So follow the way of Abraham, the upright. He was not among the polytheists.*'" (Al 'Imran 3: 93–95) The present practice of the Jewish community not to combine meat and milk, and to use non-dairy creamers instead of milk in coffee, has no basis in the Torah.

The frequent reference to Ibrahim, while inviting the People of the Book for a dialogue, indicates that the Qur'anic dialogical approach is to proceed from what is common to where differences exist. The strongest common ground is the *tawhidic* conduct and behaviour through the teachings of Ibrahim. The above narrative of the Qur'an makes it clear that it wants to identify a common ground between the teachings of the Final Messenger ﷺ and the faith of the People of the Book who claim to follow the path of Ibrahim, Ishaq and Musa.

Shirk, or associating partners with Allah, is not limited to worship. When a priest declares something permissible (*halal*) or prohibited (*haram*), he actually exercises authority in a domain which belongs only to Allah.

Three Commonalities

After establishing the fact that Islam is essentially the *tawhidic* faith of Ibrahim, other common features are traced, such as the common place of worship—the first House of Allah built by Ibrahim and Isma'il as the common *qiblah*. The Qur'an calls the place where Ibrahim used to pray as an *ayah* or sign of Allah's Authority, and orders to take the place where he stood when erecting the Kabah as a place of prayer. Therefore, the Kabah he built is to be faced when making the five daily obligatory prayers.

The Qur'an also refers to misconceptions in the minds of the Christians and the Jews regarding the construction of Sulayman's Temple in Quds. Historically, the Temple was built by Prophet Dawud [David] and Sulayman [Solomon] several centuries after Ibrahim and Musa. As the Kabah was declared the House of Allah by Ibrahim, it was customary among the Jewish people to face towards the Kabah when they made any special prayer.

POINT TO PONDER

The Bani Isra'il knew well that the House of Allah in Makkah was built by their great-grandfather Prophet Ibrahim and his son, Isma'il —long before the construction of the Temple by Prophets Dawud and Sulayman—as the first place of worshiping Allah on Earth. Therefore, facing towards Makkah while praying was not a deviation but a revival of the original practice of Ibrahim and Isma'il which was also followed by the progeny of Ibrahim till the construction of the Temple in Jerusalem .

The First House of Worship

The Qur'an, thus, makes the issue of the first House of worship abundantly clear: "*Behold! The first House [of prayer] established for mankind is the one at Bakkah [Makkah]:it is full of blessing and is a centre of guidance for the whole world. In it, there are Clear Signs and the station of Abraham; whoever enters it becomes secure. Pilgrimage to the House of Allah is a duty owed to Allah by all who can afford their way to it. As for those who refuse to follow His commands, surely Allah stands in need of no one in the whole universe.*

Say: O People of the Book! Why do you reject the Signs of Allah when Allah is witness to all that you do?' Say: O People of the Book! Why do you hinder believers from the way of Allah, seeking that they follow a crooked way, even though you yourself are witness to its being the Right Way? And Allah is not heedless of what you do.'" (Al 'Imran 3: 96–99)

Historically, the Kabah was erected by Ibrahim and Isma'il around 900 years before Musa, while the Temple of Solomon was built 480 years after Musa's exodus from Egypt (Old Testament, 1: Kings, Chapter six). This establishes the fact that the Kabah was declared as the centre of worship long before the time of Musa and Sulayman. Scholars have inferred from the *ayah:* "*Recall when Abraham and Ishmael raised the foundations of the House, praying: 'Our Lord! Accept this from us. You are indeed the All-Hearing, All-Knowing,*'" (al-Baqarah 2: 127) that it means there were already some traces of the foundations laid down by Adam on which the walls of the Kabah were later erected by Ibrahim and Isma'il. The building of the Kabah, according to certain reports, was washed away during the flood in the time of Nuh. Prophets Ibrahim and Isma'il, under the guidance from Allah, located its foundations and revived the structure. Perhaps this is why the Qur'an calls it an *ayah*. All these indications in the Qur'an and authentic reports prove that the first House of worship created on Earth for all human beings was the Masjid al-Haram at Makkah.

The performance of hajj every year is also a continuation of the ritual established by Ibrahim. It is an obligation on all believers, subject to the condition of availability of resources. Therefore, if a believer has resources to travel and perform hajj yet still, without any valid reason, chooses not to observe this obligation, then he/she will be held accountable. These *ayat* not only demonstrate the importance of hajj, but also correct the Jewish historical error of claiming Quds as the *qiblah* of all Messengers of Allah.

In *Surah al-Baqarah*, the ideological leadership of mankind was transferred from the House of Ishaq to the House of Isma'il because the Bani Isra'il failed to observe the teachings and the role model of Musa. The task given to the Final Messenger ﷺ of Allah was to revive the Abrahamic faith and practice in full, while at the same time, function as a seal of the Prophets, bringing to termination the chain of the Prophets of God. This was possible simply because the content of the Qur'anic teachings was written down and fully preserved in the lifetime of the Messenger ﷺ. The Qur'an was also preserved in the memory of, not just a few *Sahabah* during the time of the Prophet ﷺ, but also millions of believers since then who have committed to reciting passages of revelation five times a day, without failure or lapse of time in the fifteen centuries of Islamic existence. Added to this is the fact that the whole of the Qur'an is audited every year during Ramadan, in congregation and in private gatherings, in every corner of the world wherever Muslims exist. This leaves no possibility of any variation, loss, or addition of even a single dot in the text of the Qur'an. Researchers have even documented how many words, commas and periods are in the Qur'anic text.

The House of worship and its surroundings are declared by the above *ayat* as a peace zone, a protected area in which not only human life but even animal life is sacred. No one is allowed to carry firearms or any weapons in the area, and anyone who enters the area is promised safety and peace. Those who violate the peace and security of this House of worship are condemned. The Qur'an also declares the boundaries of the Haram to be restricted to the believers, while the *mushrikin* are prohibited to enter the area—not because of their colour, race, or ethnicity—but only because of their *shirk*, which is deemed inappropriate for the sanctity of the Haram.

The Behavioural Outcome of Attachment to Allah Through Hajj

Whoever attaches himself/herself to Allah alone by leaving behind friends, relatives, and national affiliations, and seeks *i'tisam billah* (holding fast to Allah), will no doubt, undergo major behavioural changes. When a person decides to perform hajj, he/she leaves his/her homeland, national dress, language, and business activities, and travels thousands of miles to reach the House of Allah. His/her objective is not one of religious tourism, rather one of detaching oneself from all attachments with family, profession, society and their social circle—solely to visit the House of Allah as His honoured guests, and to physically prove his/her love for Him by performing the rites He has prescribed, such as, the *tawaf*, *sa'i* and *wuquf al-'Arafat*. After the completion of *tawaf*, a believer tries to stay as close to the walls of the Kabah as possible and renews the pledge of obedience between tears, sobs and prayers.

Dimensions of the Word *Ayah*

The word used to show the significance of the Kabah as the first House of Allah and as a symbol of the uncompromising Unity (*tawhid*) and Uniqueness of Allah is: *ayah*. It points towards and is a reminder of a history forgotten by the Bani Isra'il. They did not remember that it was their patriarch who erected the Kabah on its foundations. They only remembered the Temple of Solomon and David—Sulayman and Dawud—as a reminder of their past glory.

The word *ayah* (pl. *ayat*), used in its various derivations in around 385 places in the Qur'an, carries several meanings such as: sign, token, mark, miracle, wonder, marvel, example, model and pointer.

First and foremost, the word *ayah* refers to the verses in the Qur'an, which are conveyed through their proper recitation by the Prophet ﷺ, "*Allah did confer a great favour on the believers when He sent among them a messenger from among themselves, reciting unto them the ayat of Allah [i.e., the Qur'an], purifying them and teaching them the Book and Wisdom, while before that they had been in manifest error.*" (Al 'Imran 3: 164) A similar message appears in *Surah al-Baqarah* 2: 129 and 2: 151, and in *Surah al-Jumu'ah* 62: 2.

The uniqueness (*i'jaz*) of the Qur'an lies in the fact that every single *ayah* has been revealed with an open invitation to anyone, Arab or non-Arab, to come forward and produce a statement similar to it. This is why every single *ayah* is evidence to the transcendence of the Qur'an as Allah's Speech, as a unique message full of wisdom, and as something beyond the capacity of any human being to reproduce.

The word *ayah* is also used to refer to a miraculous occurrence which only Allah can create, and no individual or group of people can. The creation of Adam from dust and, with Allah's Command, his becoming a living human being with all faculties and vital organs working in their best form; and the creation of his mate, both are *ayat* of Allah's Power, Planning, and Ability to do things in a manner so perfect that no one else can replicate, "*One of His signs [ayat] is that He created you from dust, then—behold!—you are human beings spreading over [the Earth]. And one of His signs [ayat] is that He created for you spouses from among yourselves so that you may find comfort in them.*" (al-Rum 30: 20–21)

In the story of 'Isa: his birth without a father, his talking from the cradle, and later on, his making of birds from clay and, with Allah's Command or *kalimah*, letting those very birds fly, are *ayat* of the truthfulness of 'Isa's Prophethood and his message of *tawhid*, "*...And he will be a Messenger to the Children of Israel. [And when he came to them he said]: 'I have come to you* *with a sign [ayah] from your Lord. I will make for you from clay the likeness of a bird and then I will breathe into it, and by the leave of Allah, it will become a bird.'"* (Al 'Imran 3: 49)

In the Qur'anic narrative of Musa: When he approaches Pharaoh and lets him know that he was designated as a Messenger by Allah *Rabb al-'alamin*, Pharoah questioned him as to who *Rabb al-'alamin* (Lord of the worlds) was and what evidence (*ayah*) he had of being appointed as Allah's Messenger, *"[Pharaoh] said: 'If you have come with a Sign [ayah], then bring it, if what you say is true.'"* (al-A'raf 7: 106)

The Qur'an also uses the word *ayah* with reference to the creation and functioning of the universe: the alternation of day and night; the movement of the sun, moon and stars; the role of mountains, rivers and oceans; the benefits human beings receive from the animal world and vegetations; change of climates, and so on: *"Surely, in the creation of the heavens and the earth, and alternation of night and day, there are Signs [ayat] for persons of understanding."* (Al 'Imran 3: 190)

There are remarkable signs in, not only the universe, but also within every human being, for those who investigate, use reason, ponder and think critically, *"Soon shall We show them Our Signs [ayat] in the universe and in their own selves until it becomes manifest to them that this is the Truth."* (Fussilat 41: 53)

Every single species of animal, bird, fish and fruit even insects, is an evidence or *ayah* of Allah's love, compassion, care, and concern for the betterment of human beings and their healthy living, *"He it is Who sends down water for you from the sky out of which you drink and out of which grow the plants on which you pasture your cattle. With it He produces for you [various] crops, olives, date palms, grapes and all kinds of fruit. Surely, in this there is a great Sign [ayah] for those who reflect."* (al-Nahl 16: 10–11)

The word *ayah* also refers to the ruins of earlier nations who violated the directions of Allah and the teachings of His Messengers. The ruins of great architectural monuments built by the people of 'Ad, Thamud, Lut, Salih, and Shu'ayb are an indication and pointer for those who want to take lessons from the history of evil-doers.

The design and function of vital limbs and parts of the human body are *ayat* of Allah's perfect creation (*ahsan taqwim*) of the human body. They are evidence to prove that human beings are not by-products of a blind biological process of evolution; rather that they are created in their own right, in the best possible mould, by the One and Only Creator who does not need to go through a process of trial and error to ultimately make human beings.

Some chronicled events, which changed the direction of history are also called *ayat* by the Qur'an: "*Indeed, there was a sign (ayah) for you in the two armies that met in battle—one fighting for the cause of Allah and the other in denial. The believers saw their enemy twice their number. But Allah supports with His victory whomever He wills. Surely, in this is a lesson for people of insight.*" (Al 'Imran 3: 13)

Similarly, at another place the Qur'an mentions: "*Say [O Prophet]: 'O People of the Book! Why do you reject the Signs [ayat] of Allah when Allah is witness to all that you do?' Say: 'O People of the Book! Why do you hinder believers from the way of Allah, seeking that they follow a crooked way even though you yourselves are witness to its being the Right Way? And Allah is not heedless of what you do. O believers! Were you to obey a party of those who were given the Book, they might cause you to renounce the Truth after you have attained to faith. How can you disbelieve when you are the ones to whom the Signs [ayat] of Allah are recited and when His Messenger is in your midst? Whoever holds fast to Allah will certainly be guided to the Straight Path [sirat al-mustaqim].'*" (Al 'Imran 3: 98–101)

Earlier, Jews were reminded about their unbecoming behaviour of not only opposing the truth but trying to revive pre-Islamic rivalries between the two major tribes of the Ansar, namely the Aws and the Khazraj. In one instance Samar ibn Qays, a Jew, was able to rouse tribal enmity between both the tribes and they were on the verge of starting a fight among themselves. When the Prophet ﷺ heard about it, he rushed to them in order to dissuade the clash. Specifically speaking, the *ayah* refers to this situation. However, in a more general sense, it is relevant for Muslims even today. The conflict between the Muslim countries in the Middle East is evidence to this phenomenon. To exploit disunity amongst Muslims a deep-rooted divide between the Arabs and others was created by known Jewish lobbyists involved in the movement of Arab nationalism, thus further division was created to weaken them.

Surah al-Hujurat makes it an obligation on the believers to make peace (*sulh*) between members of society: "*If two parties of the believers happen to fight, make peace between them. But then, if one of them transgresses against the other, fight the one that transgresses, until it reverts to Allah's command. And if it does revert, make peace between them with justice, and be equitable, for Allah loves the equitable. Surely, the believers are none but brothers unto one another, so set things right between your brothers. And have fear of Allah that you may be shown mercy.*" (al-Hujurat 49: 9–10)

The Leadership Role of the Muslims

Holding fast to the cable or rope of Allah (Al 'Imran 3: 103) is the key to success for the Muslims as one *ummah*. In the Battle of Badr, believers saw how Allah helped His sincere servants. However, not all people have the same capacities in all human societies. Capacity-building, therefore, becomes the critical need of every society. Allah wants the Muslim *ummah* to have continuous assessment of its capacity, planning and performance. The Qur'an confers the Muslim *ummah* with the role of leadership over all nations of the world. Therefore, it is incumbent upon the *ummah* to take practical steps and develop an appropriate strategy so as to present a holistic model of Islamic *da'wah*—that of peace, love, sacrifice and obedience to Allah. Muslims should become leaders in knowledge, socio-economic developments and fair, just governance.

The message is conveyed in simple words: "*O Believers! Fear Allah as He should be feared, and do not die save in submission to Allah. Hold fast together to the cable of Allah, [i.e., the Qur'an], and be not divided. Remember Allah's favour upon you when you were once enemies, then He brought your hearts together, so that—through His blessings—you became brothers. You stood on the brink of a pit of fire and He delivered you from it. Thus, Allah makes His Signs [ayat] clear to you that you may be guided to the Right Way.*

Let there be a party among you who will call [people] to all that is good [khayr], enjoin the doings of all that is right [ma'ruf], and forbid the doing of all that is wrong [munkar]—it is they who will be successful. Do not be like those who fell into factions and became opposed to one another after Clear Signs [bayyinat] had come to them. It is they who will suffer a mighty punishment. On that Day, some faces will turn bright and other faces will turn dark. Those whose faces have turned dark will be told: 'Did you not fall into unbelief after you had been blessed with belief? So taste the punishment for your unbelief.' And those whose faces have turned bright, they will be in the mercy of Allah, and therein they shall abide forever. These are the messages [ayat] of Allah which We recite to you in all truth. And Allah desires no wrong to the [people of the] worlds. To Allah belongs all that is in the heavens and the earth, and to Allah are all matters returned for decision." (Al 'Imran 3: 102–109)

Faith, Unity and Ethical Role of the Muslims

Believers are reminded to observe *taqwa* to the best of their capacity [*haqq*]. 'Abdullah ibn Mas'ud narrates: "*Haqq* of *taqwa* means obedience to Allah in everything. No act should be in violation of Allah's obedience while remembering Him and—without any failing—offer gratefulness to Him." God-consciousness is directly linked with a person's attachment to the Qur'an, as the *ayah* uses the word *hablillah* (the rope or cable of Allah), referring to the Qur'an. The Qur'an is the cementing force between the hearts and minds of the believers. God-consciousness and complete attachment to the Qur'an transforms the believers into an *ummah* with a mission, a purpose, and a goal.

The *ummah* or the Muslim community is commissioned to play a leadership role in guiding human beings to what is good (*ma'ruf*) and stopping them from doing all unethical and wrong things (*munkar*).

The use of the word *ya'muruna* indicates that it is not a matter of just preaching what is good, but a matter of commanding, directing, implementing and doing one's utmost for the realization of an ethical and moral change in the behaviour and attitude of the people: individuals, society as well as the state. Therefore, believers are obliged to use all possible resources towards the fulfillment of *amr bi al-ma'ruf* and *nahi 'an al-munkar*. Every believer, individually and collectively, is accountable in front of Allah for this responsibility.

This also implies that *da'wah* is a call for realization of an ethical order which demands change, not just at an individual level, but also at the institutional and governance levels. *Da'wah* plays an effective role in the dissemination of the message of truth, peace, honesty and justice in society. It is in this sense that Allah informed the angels that He is going to place His vicegerents (*khalifah*) on earth, who shall establish truth and justice in society.

Muslims are clearly told that if they play their role as the best of nations (*khayra ummah*) appropriately, then they shall qualify to be the people whose faces shall shine on the Day of Judgement, and who shall be welcomed into Paradise as their permanent abode: "*Do not lose heart or grieve; for you shall surely gain the upper hand if you are true believers.*" (Al 'Imran 3: 139) But if, like some of the People of the Book, they fail in fulfilling their responsibility, they will belong to the people whose faces will be gloomy on the Day of Judgement, and they will not receive Allah's Mercy on that Day. Muslims are also warned to avoid disunity and division. They must have unity of hearts, minds and objectives.

After foretelling the believers about the good consequences of fulfilling their personal and social responsibility, the Qur'an further emphasizes that the global role of the Muslim *ummah* is dissemination and realization of the Islamic message of peace, fairness and unity among the people of the world. However, this can be materialized only when, besides having faith (*iman*) and Allah-consciousness (*taqwa*), they are also consolidated like a fortified wall; when their hearts and minds join together on the basis of *i'tisam billah*, and they are not divided into sects, pockets, linguist groups and rival parties. Believers must recall the deep rivalries they had before the advent of Islam in their lives and appreciate how, despite their hatred and enmity due to their tribalism, Islam made them one brotherhood of faith, stronger and more lasting than any blood relation. This was only due to being blessed with the *hidayah* (the Qur'an), the guidance given by their Lord, through the most kind and loving Messenger ﷺ of Allah. They were at the brink of a pit of fire, but Islam pulled them out and unified them in a loving and blessed brotherhood.

> It is also a blessing of Allah upon the Muslims that they are commissioned to become carriers of the message of peace, justice, and ethical and moral conduct, as a unified force against the forces of evil, immorality, obscenity and oppression.

They are told that their success in this world and in the life Hereafter depends on their sincere observance of practicing and enjoining good, *amr bi al-ma'ruf*, and eradicating wrong from the society, *nahi 'an al-munkar*. They are warned not to get divided after being unified through *iman*. They are also warned not to follow in the footsteps of earlier nations who preferred immediate worldly gains and lost their chance to succeed in the *Akhirah*.

The Qur'an again underscores the importance of the global leadership role of the Muslims collectively as well as individually: "*You are now the best people or community [ummah] brought forth for mankind—you enjoin what is right, forbid what is wrong, and believe in Allah.*" (Al 'Imran 3: 110)

The Qur'an assures the believers that so long as they remain faithful to Allah and do *amr bi al-ma'ruf* and *nahi 'an al-munkar* in its true spirit, their enemies shall never succeed. Ultimately, the forces of good (*ma'ruf*) are bound to prevail over the forces of evil (*munkar*) even if the latter is ten times greater in numbers, "*Had the People of the Book believed, it would have been better for them. Some of them are believers, but most of them are transgressors. They will not be able to harm you except for a little hurt, and if they fight against you they will turn their backs [in flight] and they will have no helpers. They will be stricken with disgrace wherever they go, except when they are protected by either a covenant with Allah or a covenant with men. They are laden with the burden of Allah's wrath, and humiliation has been pitched upon them. This is because they rejected the Signs [ayat] of Allah and slew the Prophets without justification, and because they wantonly disobeyed and used to transgress.*

Yet all are not alike; among the People of the Book, there are upright people who recite the messages [ayat] of Allah throughout the night, prostrating [in worship]. They believe in Allah and in the Last Day, enjoin what is right and forbid what is wrong, and race with one other in doing good. These are among the righteous [salihin]. Whatever good they do, shall never go unappreciated. Allah fully knows those who are pious. As for those who denied the Truth, neither their possessions nor their children will avail them against Allah. They are the people of the Fire, and therein they shall abide forever." (Al 'Imran 3: 110–116)

Some Implications of *Khayra Ummah*

Holding fast to the rope (*habl*) or the Book of guidance simply means full adherence to the teachings of the Qur'an. The Prophetic elaboration of the word 'rope' in the *ayah* in his famous last sermon in hajj, endorses this view: "*I have left with you two things; so long as you hold to them strongly, you will never be misguided: [they are] kitabullah [the Book of Allah] and Sunnah of the Messenger of Allah.*" "Holding fast" therefore, simply means obeying the Prophet ﷺ and the Qur'an, "*And obey Allah and His Messenger, and do not quarrel with one another lest you should lose courage and your power departs. Be steadfast! Surely, Allah is with those who remain steadfast.*" (al-Anfal 8: 46)

The *ayah* 104 of *Surah Al 'Imran* provides a clear vision of the global *da'wah* responsibility: a collective as well as individual obligation of the believers, "*Let there be a party among you who will call [people] to all that is good [khayr], enjoin the doing of all that is right [ma'ruf], and forbid the doing of all that is wrong [munkar].*" (Al 'Imran 3: 104)

This ethical and legal responsibility upon believers, individually and collectively, is a recurring theme in the Qur'an. It is repeated in slightly different words a bit later in the same *surah* (*ayah* 110), which reinforces the importance of the mission of the Muslim community, both in a Muslim-majority context as well as one where Muslims may not be in a majority.

The terms used, *khayr, ma'ruf* and *munkar*, are defined by the Qur'an itself. The word *khayr* means goodness, excellence, a good thing, a blessing in the form of wealth or knowledge, or an act of charity. It is the opposite of *sharr* which means evil, mischief, calamity, disaster, wickedness and malice. *Khayr* refers to things which bring benefit to the people. It is used frequently in the Qur'an in different contexts. For example, in the context of warfare, it is said: "*Fighting is ordained upon you though it is disliked by you. Perhaps you dislike a thing even though it is good [khayr] for you...*" (al-Baqarah 2: 216) It also refers to all good and rewarding deeds: "*whoever voluntarily does more good (khayra) than is required, will find it better for him."* (al-Baqarah 2: 184) It is also used for the best strategy adopted by Allah: *"And they schemed, but Allah countered their schemes [by a scheme of His own]. Allah is the best [khayrun] of schemers."* (Al 'Imran 3: 54)

The word *ma'ruf* comes from the root letters *'a-r-f* which means to know, to recognize, to perceive. It also means what is well known, universally recognized, and generally accepted. It refers to all ethical and good deeds. The opposite of *ma'ruf* is *munkar*. Its root letters are *n-k-r* which means refusing to know, to deny, disagreeable, objectionable, detestable and acts disapproved by society. Obscenity for example is *munkar*, *"Surely, Allah enjoins justice ['adl], kindness [ihsan] and the doing of good to kith and kin. He forbids all that is shameful [fahsha]), evil [munkar] and oppressive."* (al-Nahl 16: 90)

The comprehensive message conveyed in this *ayah* is to avoid all prohibited things which fall in the category of *fahash* or *munkar*. *Fahash* includes all lewd behaviours, such as exposing parts of the body which are supposed to be covered and use of vulgar language or gestures. Islam persuades believers to observe their social and moral obligation towards the realization of *'adl* and respectful and generous attitude towards parents, relatives, neighbours and even strangers. In fact, being kind towards kith and kin is an indication of the observance of *'adl* and *ihsan* at the individual and societal levels.

The words used in *ayah* 104, *"Let there be a party among you who will call [people] to all that is good [khayr], enjoin the doing of all that is right [ma'ruf], and forbid the doing of all that is wrong [munkar]—it is they who will be successful,"* calls for special consideration. It defines the Muslim *ummah*'s mission as *da'wah*, i.e., inviting humanity towards the path of good (*ma'ruf*), truth (*sidq*), trust (*amanah*), fairness (*'adl*), beautiful conduct and behaviour (*taqwa*) and seeking Allah's pleasure (*rida*).

The root word *da'a* means to call or invite; *da'wah* means invitation; and the *da'i* is the person who invites. Calling people towards good (*khayr*) as mentioned in the above *ayah* of *Al 'Imran* has been the common mission of all Prophets of Allah. For example, Nuh said: *"My Lord! I called [da'watu] my people by night and by day, but the more I called the farther they fled.*" (Nuh 71: 5–6)

The Prophets of Allah call people to the Path of Allah, while Satan calls people to the path of misguidance (*dalalah*). After having diverted people from the Right Path in this world, Satan will say in his defense on the Day of Judgement: "*Surely, whatever Allah promised you was true; as for me, I went back on the promise I made to you. I had no power over you except I called you [da'watukum] to my way and you responded to me.*" (Ibrahim 14: 22) Satan makes his *da'wah* attractive with worldly pleasures which leads to Allah's displeasure and punishment. *Da'wah* towards good (*khayr*) and beautiful deeds (*hasanat*) has been made an obligation on all believing men and women. They are advised to establish the *din* and present it to human beings in the most beautiful manner. It is the message of peace (*aman*), love (*hubb*) and servitude to Allah (*'ubudiyyah*). But as the Qur'an says, there is no compulsion (*ikrah*) or use of force in Islamic *da'wah*: "*There is no compulsion [ikrah] in religion. The Right Way stands clearly distinguished from the wrong. Hence, whoever rejects the false gods and believes in Allah has indeed taken hold of the firm unshakable handle.*" (al-Baqarah 2: 256)

The first step needed for *da'wah* is to understand and internalize the comprehensive Qur'anic message of total ethical transformation of personality: "*And who is better in speech than he who calls [da'a] to Allah, acts righteously, and says: 'I am a Muslim'?*" (Fussilat 41: 33) *Da'wah* begins with one's own conscious acceptance, and becoming a role model of obedience to Allah. The role model itself becomes an invitation for people to see what kind of behavioural change Islam brings in a believer. But *da'wah* is not to be confined to one's own good behaviour; the beauty of Islam and its blessings are to be shared with others too, "*Call to the way of your Lord with wisdom and goodly exhortation, and reason with them in the best manner possible.*" (al-Nahl 16: 125)

The *ayat* 104 and 110 of *Surah Al 'Imran* place enormous responsibility on the *ummah* to present itself as a role model to the people of the world.

It is not a privilege of the clergy or ordained religious leaders, as there is no concept of clergy in Islam. Every believing man and woman is supposed to be a carrier of Islamic *da'wah*. Similarly, the Islamic state is not a value-neutral institution, and it is also obliged to do *da'wah*.

Muslims as a Qualitative Community

The message conveyed in *ayah* 110 is obvious; Muslims are called *khayra ummah*, meaning the best community, not due to their having natural resources, being large in number, or having the best scientists and mathematicians, but for one reason alone: that they enjoin what is universally known as good (*ma'ruf*), virtuous, ethical and fair and they forbid what is bad, unethical and harmful. This task of *da'wah* is more than verbal communication of the message. *Ummah* is not a hypothetical, abstract or theoretical concept; it substitutes the particularistic concept of nation with a trans-national concept of unified global Muslim community.

The obligation of an Islamic state, to put in efforts for the practical realization of an ethical order at a state level is elaborated in *Surah al-Hajj*: "*[Allah will certainly help] those who, were We to bestow authority on them in the land, will establish prayer, render alms-tax [zakah], enjoin good and forbid evil. And the end of all matters rest with Allah.*" (al-Hajj 22: 41) The same concept is referred to in *Surah al-Shura*: "*Establish the din [the way of life] and do not split up regarding it.*" (al-Shura 42: 13) *Iqamah* of the *din* is more than a matter of sermonization. It means the practical realization of the Islamic way of life, and of Islamic ethical principles in social, economic, legal and political domains; in other words, the institutionalization of Islam's socio-economic and political order.

The Muslim community, therefore, must be proactive in not only the verbal communication of its message of *tawhid*, but also to take necessary steps to introduce and realistically materialize an ethical behavioural and social change within the society.

The first step in this direction, according to the Qur'an, is behavioural conformity and becoming a role model of ethical and moral conduct in one's personal, social, economic and legal matters, by following the loving example of the Prophet ﷺ: "*O Believers! Why do you profess that which you do not practice? It is greatly abhorrent in the sight of Allah that you should profess what you do not practice!*" (al-Saff 61: 2–3) The task of behavioural change in the society, therefore, begins with change in one's own self and the family, "*O believers! Guard yourselves and your families against a Fire whose fuel is human beings and stones.*" (al-Tahrim 66: 6)

These few *ayats,* 103-110, deserve repeated contemplation to grasp their essence. They remind a believer of Allah's enormous bounty on them by cementing their hearts together with the Qur'an, which is the core, and anchor of faith for every Muslim and Muslimah. This unity of faith, mind and heart transforms the physical existence of the Muslims into an ideological and message-oriented single body (*khyra ummah*) whose objective becomes a career of calling to ethicalize conduct, behaviour, thinking, feelings on *ma'ruf* in order to bring an ethical revolution in human life, society and community. This task of establishing good *ma'ruf* and eradicating evil, corruption, injustice, obscenity and wrong (*munkar*) is so noble that all those who join their hands in it are called by the Qur'an *khyra ummah*. They are the salt of earth. They are the cream of society. Their being less in number does not bother them. Their qualitative impact is deeper than their quantitative count.

It is also a truism that throughout human history there has always remained a small number of people who may be confused or misled by their selfishness and the misguidance of Satan to look for short term gains, immediate benefits and forget their long-term benefits. The hypocrites (*munafiqun*) and the polytheists (*mushrikun*) share in this attitude of mind.

Their mindset makes them defaulters and they excel in *fisq*, disobedience of the One Who gave them life, capacities and resources.

The Qur'an mentions that they cannot harm the Prophet ﷺ, nor those who later stand for truth. They only harm themselves and a chastisement waits them in the life Hereafter.

Those who denied the Truth, they shall face disrespect in this world and in the life Hereafter. The wealth, power and authority they enjoyed in the world and their children for whom they indulged in corruption, none of them will be of any help. They are bound to face punishment for their unethical and evil behaviour in this worldly life. A beautiful simile is used by the Qur'an to illustrate their ultimate destiny: "*The example of what they spend in the life of this world is like that of a wind accompanied with frost which smote the harvest of a people who wronged themselves, and laid it to waste. It is not Allah Who wronged them rather it is they who wronged themselves.*" (Al 'Imran 3: 117)

Outcomes of *Da'wah*

All those who are more knowledgeable about the Qur'an, the Prophetic Sunnah, and Islamic disciplines (*'ulum*) must share their knowledge and experience with their fellow Muslims and the members of the global community. Those in authority in a Muslim state are equally responsible for the implementation of what is good and removal of what is evil. Media and educational institutions must play a constructive role in creating awareness and in the realization of a culture of modesty (*haya*), peace, honesty, fulfillment of covenants, truthfulness, family values and observing social responsibility.

Those who perform this dynamic and creative role are defined by the Qur'an as persons who shall have radiant faces on the Day of Judgement, while those who fail to do so will have dark and gloomy faces. Muslims are also warned to watch out for falling into the trap of sectarianism, as it happened with earlier nations, more specifically among the followers of Judaism and Christianity. Sectarianism destroys the unity and solidarity of a community and frustrates all venues of progress and development.

In a materialistic society, generally, economic progress and development are the basis of social interaction and friendship. The Qur'an, however, looks at friendship from the viewpoint of faith. All those who believe in Allah and the Final Messenger ﷺ are declared by the Qur'an as a single brotherhood or a fraternity, "*Indeed, the believers are one brotherhood.*" (al-Hujurat 49:10) Their basis of friendship, mutual trust and solidarity is their common faith. Believers are advised to develop intimate friendship only with their brothers in faith. Naturally, common sense demands that those who were identified as hypocrites could not be taken as friends, "*O Believers! Do not take as intimate friends those who are not your kind. They spare nothing to ruin you. Indeed, they long for you to suffer. Their interest is clearly manifest in what they say—and what their breasts conceal is even greater. We have made Our message clear to you, if only you can understand. Lo! It is you who love them, but they do not love you, even though you believe in all the scriptures. When they meet you, they say, 'We believe,' but when they are by themselves, they bite their fingers in rage at you. Say: 'Perish in your rage!' Allah knows even what lies hidden in their breasts.*" (Al 'Imran 3: 118–119)

While advising the believers as to whom they should choose for trusted friends, the Qur'an illustrates its point by referring to the enmity of the People of the Book and the hypocrites (*munafiqun*) towards the believers. In a critical situation such as in Uhud, the leader of the *munafiqun,* 'Abdullah ibn Ubayy, withdrew three hundred of his men; and the Muslims were left with only seven hundred men against three thousand of the *mushrikin*.

With special help from Allah, a small number of the believers defeated the well-equipped large number of the *mushrikin* of Makkah. The lessons learnt were at least three. First, in the conflict between truth and falsehood, the key factor is neither the head count, nor the strength of equipment and armaments, but the trust in Allah, in whose Name the war is waged. Second,

Allah is All-Aware of such situations, and He has His own ways of providing help to the believers. Third, believers should never count on the promises of hidden enemies of the believers, for they could betray the Muslims at any point in time. The *munafiqun*, by definition, are never sincere to the believers: "*If anything good happens to you, they are grieved; if any misfortune befalls you, they rejoice. Yet if you remain steadfast and mindful of Allah, their designs will not cause you any harm. Allah surely encompasses all that they do. [O Messenger, remind the Muslims of the occasion] when you went forth from your home at early dawn (to the battlefield of Uhud) and placed the believers in battle arrays. Allah is All-Hearing, All-Knowing. And (recall) when two groups from among you were inclined to lose heart, although Allah was their Protector. So, in Allah let the believers put their trust. Indeed, Allah helped you at Badr when you were utterly weak. So be mindful of Allah, perhaps you will be thankful.*" (Al 'Imran 3: 120–123)

The take-home point for not only the believers but the whole of mankind, who are the addressee of the Qur'an, is that, with total sincerity to our Creator, if we stand for truth, justice and fairness, piety always prevails over evil and corruption.

The believers are reminded that if they are sincere and trust in Allah's help, they shall never be abandoned by Him: "*And [recall, O Prophet] when you said to the believers: 'Will it not suffice you that your Lord will aid you by sending down three thousand angels?' Surely, if you are steadfast and mindful of Allah, and the enemy should suddenly fall upon you, your Lord will help you with five thousand marked angels. Allah has reminded you of this only as a glad tiding to you and to let your hearts be at rest. Help can only come from Allah, the Almighty, the All-Wise. [Allah provided this aid to you] in order that He may cut asunder a part of those who disbelieved or frustrate them so that they retreat in utter disappointment.*" (Al 'Imran 3: 124–127)

The way in which the *munafiqun* of Madinah betrayed the Prophet ﷺ and the *Sahabah* was devastating and shocking. But the Prophet ﷺ, being full of compassion and mercy, still worried about how to save those who were at the brink of the pit of fire. Aware of the soft-heartedness of the Prophet ﷺ, the Qur'an advises: "*[O Messenger!] You have no part of the authority [to decide] whether He will accept their repentance or chastise them; for they surely are wrongdoers. To Allah belongs whatever is in the heavens and the earth. He forgives whomever He wills, and chastises whomever He wills. And Allah is All-Forgiving, Most Merciful.*" (Al 'Imran 3: 128–129)

The Culture of *Ma'ruf* and Elimination of Social Evils

Surah Al 'Imran provides a unique thematic continuity on major social issues that were touched upon in *Surah al-Baqarah*. Interestingly, the treatment of these themes is always gelled together with matters of belief (*aqidah*), and reward in the *Akhirah*. Both *surahs* (*al-Baqarah* and *Al 'Imran*) enlighten the reader on Allah's enormous Mercy (*rahmah*), Forgiveness (*maghfirah*) and Pardon (*'afuww*) towards His people. Every breach of the covenant by the People of the Book provided enough ground to make a final verdict against them and annihilate them. But His *rahmah* always prevails over His displeasure and allows even the defaulters opportunity to return to Him, mend their ways and seek His forgiveness. Normally, Satan's strategy is to distance a believer from his Lord through traps of wealth and greed, sexual attractions, or ethnic and racial pride. These are well known tricks used by Satan who does his best to misguide even the who fear Allah.

In *Surah al-Baqarah*, *riba* or all forms of interest were declared, prohibited, *haram*. The Qur'an further elaborates on certain confusions created by satanic intelligence, for example, that the real intent behind the prohibition of *riba* is to discourage multiple interest which may be unfair, but simple interest is fine as it is only a service charge! The Qur'an categorically declares all forms of interest to be prohibited: "*O Believers! Do not devour interest, doubled and redoubled, and be mindful of Allah so that you may attain true success. Have fear of the Fire which awaits those who deny the Truth. Obey Allah and the Messenger, so that mercy be shown to you."* (Al 'Imran 3: 130–132)

POINT TO PONDER

Interest (*riba*) is a grave financial and social exploitation, and an oppression of the poor by the rich. The Qur'an condemns and prohibits both simple as well as compound forms of interest. It warns everyone involved in interest of a severe chastisement: "*And have fear of the Fire which awaits those who deny the Truth. And obey Allah and the Messenger, so that mercy may be shown to you.*" (Al 'Imran 3: 131–132)

An observation of over fifty years of the performance of the global agencies who, under strict conditions, gave loans to the developing countries, proves that no country that took such a loan ever become self-sufficient in its economy, nor could it repay its total loan. It hardly managed to repay the service charges while making requests to extend the time frame of the loan.

POINT TO PONDER

The beauty of the Qur'an is that, after cautioning a person about the serious consequences of violation of Allah's commands and the Prophet's instructions, it keeps inviting every wrong doer towards the open door of Allah's Mercy and forgiveness. This door never closes. It is only the misfortune of a defaulter if he/she does not rush to seek Allah's blessings and *maghfirah*.

The wordings used in the Qur'an overflow with compassion, love and concern of the Lord for His servants, and shows His keenness to accept repentance and generously pardon even habitual violators, if only they choose to return to Him. If they move one step towards Him, He moves ten steps towards them to forgive and shower His Mercy on them: "*And hasten to the forgiveness of your Lord and to the Paradise as vast as the heavens and the earth, prepared for the God-fearing. [They are those] who spend in the way of Allah both in affluence and in hardship, who restrain their anger, and forgive others. Allah loves such good-doers. [These are the ones] who, when they commit any indecency or wrong themselves, instantly remember Allah and implore forgiveness for their sins—for who will forgive sins save Allah? – and do not willfully persist in the wrong they had committed. They shall be recompensed by forgiveness from their Lord and by Gardens beneath which rivers flow; there they shall abide. How good is the reward of those who work [righteously]! Many eras have passed before you, travel through the land and behold the end of those who rejected [the directives and commands of Allah]. This is a plain exposition for mankind—and a guidance and admonition for the Allah-fearing.*" (Al 'Imran 3: 133–138)

Every single word of the Qur'an speaks for Allah's Mercy, Love and enormous forgiveness for whoever comes back to Him. Only the most unfortunate and misguided would miss such a raincheck—an offer to get redeemed without any intercession.

How loving, kind and forgiving Allah is, this is further illustrated in the following *ayat*, which apparently is a critique of a Muslim contingent in the Battle of Uhud for not following the Prophet's instructions to watch the mountain pass behind the Muslim forces. This lapse on the part of the Muslims cost them heavily in terms of loss of life and in terms of the transformation of an evident victory into a highly confused situation. Nevertheless, the *mushrikin* felt that they had taken their revenge and left the war field to return to Makkah. The Prophet ﷺ, with his foresight and knowledge of war tactics, asked a contingent of cavalry to follow the Makkans so that it would send across the message that the Muslims are not weak and are ready for another encounter: "*Do not lose heart or grieve, for you shall surely gain the upper hand if you are [steadfast] believers. If you have suffered a wound [at Uhud], the people opposed to you have suffered a similar wound [at Badr]. We alternate these days [of victory and defeat] among people so that Allah might mark out those who [truly] believe, and select from among you those who [really] bear witness [to the Truth]—and Allah does not love the wrongdoers—and He makes men go through trials in order that He might purge the believers and destroy the disbelievers. Did you think that you would enter Paradise even though Allah has not yet seen who among you strove hard [in His Way] and remained steadfast? You previously longed for death [in the way of Allah], now you have faced it, observing it with your own eyes.*" (Al 'Imran 3: 139–143)

Believers are asked to reflect on the ways that Allah deals with His servants. Success, hardships and failures, all are meant to objectively measure the believers' state of *iman, taqwa,* and *istiqamah*. In the case of Uhud, instead of following the fleeing Makkans as the Prophet ﷺ had directed, they started to collect the spoils of war—a sign of immediacy and not of ultimacy. This sent the wrong message to the contingent placed by the Prophet ﷺ at a strategic defense post, that perhaps the war is over and that they may also join in collecting spoils of war. Khalid ibn al-Walid, who was leading the troops of Makkans, found a strategic opportunity to harm the Muslims and attacked them from behind when they were mentally not prepared to face this situation. This changed a great victory into a confused situation in which the Muslims, not only lost valuable lives, but the Prophet ﷺ himself also got injured and a rumor was spread that he had been martyred. This added to the Muslim troop's pain, and they became depressed to the extent that a leading *Sahabi* commented that if the Prophet was martyred, then there was no need to fight any further. Another *Sahabi* responded that if the Prophet ﷺ was martyred, then they *must* fight, more vigorously, in fact, till they also achieve martyrdom, because there is no meaning to life without the Prophet ﷺ in their midst.

The Qur'an comments on this confused situation: "*Muhammad is no more than a Messenger, and Messengers have passed away before him. Then if he were to die or be slain, will you turn about on your heels? Whoever turns about on his heels can in no way harm Allah. As for the grateful ones, Allah will soon reward them.*" (Al 'Imran 3: 144)

A more detailed post-Uhud analysis is done by the Qur'an from the perspective of the conflict between the upholders of Truth on one hand and the forces of *kufr*, *taghut* and *shirk* on the other, and the expected role of the steadfast believers: "*No soul can ever die except with the leave of Allah and at an appointed time. He who desires his reward in this world, We shall grant it to him; and he who desires the reward of the Hereafter, We shall grant it to him. And soon shall We reward those that are grateful.*

Many were the Prophets on whose side fought a large number of people devoted to Allah; they neither lost heart for all they had to suffer in the way of Allah nor did they weaken or abase themselves. Allah loves the patient ones.

And all they said was: 'Our Lord! Forgive us our sins and our excesses in our affairs, set our feet firm, and grant us victory against those who deny the Truth.' Thereupon, Allah granted them the reward of this world and the excellent reward of the Hereafter. Allah loves those who do good." (Al 'Imran 3: 145–148)

While persuading believers to follow the path of steadfastness (*istiqamah*), they are at the same time, cautioned not to fall into the trap of the unbelievers and lose trust in Allah: "*O Believers! If you follow those who deny the Truth, they will drive you back on your heels and you will turn about, losers. But Allah is the only Protector and the best of Helpers.*" (Al 'Imran 3: 149–150)

Allah has His own ways of supporting those who fight in order to establish His *din* and realize law and order on Earth. One of His ways is to cause fear and terror in the hearts of the unbelievers; consequently, despite their numerical strength and best war equipment, they feel afraid of the less-equipped and less-in-number believers. This favour of Allah was experienced by the believers, both in Badr and Uhud.

The Qur'an reminds believers that the nobility of the cause of *da'wah* and *islah* is such that they, as believers—without any consideration of their physical strength and needed war equipment—go for *jihad* with whatever they possess, relying totally on Allah. And Allah supports them with invisible powers, "*Those who say: 'Allah is our Lord,' and then remain steadfast, upon them descend angels, saying: 'Do not fear, nor grieve. Rather, receive the good tidings of Paradise which you were promised. We are your companions [helpers] in this world and in the Hereafter. There you shall have all that you desire and all what you will ask for.'*" (Fussilat 41: 30–31) With this promise of Allah, none of the believers were frightened of the enemies for their large numbers, whenever they had to encounter them: "*We will cast terror into the hearts of those who have denied the Truth since they have associated [others] with Allah [in His Divinity], for which He has sent down no sanctions. The Fire is their abode—how bad the resting place of the wrongdoers will be! Indeed, Allah surely fulfilled His promise [of victory] when you were slaying them by His leave until the moment when you flagged and quarreled among yourselves about the matter, and disobeyed the Prophet after He showed you what you intensely desire; for some of you sought this world and some of you [sought] the Next. Therefore, He turned you away from them [your foes] in order to put you to a test. Still, He pardoned you [after that]. And Allah is Gracious to those who believe.*" (Al 'Imran 3: 151–152)

Specific reference is made to the situation when the contingent of the *Sahabah* deputed to protect the mountain pass at the rear end of the *mujahidin*, left the pass unprotected because they thought the war was over and they may join others in getting the war spoils. This was a clear violation of the Prophet's directions. The Qur'an made a note of this yet at the same time gave the Muslims the benefit of the doubt, dubbing it as a confused situation. The strategic error made by the contingent led to heavy loss of life and changed the victory into a state of confusion.

"*Recall when you were fleeing without casting even a side glance at anyone, while the Messenger was calling out to you from the rear. Then Allah requited you by inflicting grief after grief upon you, so as to instruct you neither to grieve for the victory that escaped you or for the afflictions that befell you. Allah knows all that you do. Then after inflicting this grief, He sent down an inner peace upon you, a drowsiness which overtook some of you. And those who were concerned merely about themselves, entertaining false notions about Allah—the notions of the age of ignorance—asked: 'Have we any say in the matter?' Tell [them, O Prophet]: 'Truly, all power of decision rests solely with Allah.'"* (Al 'Imran 3: 153–154)

"*Indeed, they conceal in their hearts what they would not reveal to you, saying: 'If we had any power of decision, we would not have been slain here.' Say [O Prophet]: 'Even if you had been in your homes, those for whom slaying had been appointed would have gone forth to the place where they were to be slain.' [All this happened] so that Allah might test [the thoughts you entertained in] your hearts and purge your hearts [of all impurities]. Allah knows well what is in the breasts of men.*

Surely, those of them who turned their back on the day when the two armies met, [did so because] Satan made them slip because of some of their lapses. But Allah has pardoned them; He is All-Forgiving, All-Forbearing.

O Believers! Do not be like those who disbelieved and said to their brethren [who met some suffering] in the course of travelling throughout the land or [engaged in] fighting: 'Had they remained with us, they would not have died nor been slain.' Allah makes such thoughts the cause of deep regrets in their hearts. It is Allah [alone] who grants life and death. And Allah is All-Seeing of what you do.

If you were to be slain or die in the way of Allah, then surely Allah's forgiveness and mercy are better than whatever [goods] those [who stay behind] amass. Were you to die or be slain, it is to Allah that all of you will be mustered." (Al 'Imran 3: 154–158)

The Qur'an looks critically at the way some *Sahabah* behaved, yet due to Allah's Magnanimity, He overlooks the lapses of His people with an encouragement to mend their ways, and so they could qualify for *Jannah* as their destination. This is contrary to the harsh and authoritarian critique a monarch usually makes of his subjects. This is, in fact, an *ayah* or sign of Allah's limitless Mercy. This unique way of the Qur'an guides the Prophet ﷺ and whoever holds responsibility to use wisdom (*hikmah*) when correcting the behavioural issues of people in society. It also shows how the Most Merciful shows His *rahmah* to His servants so long as they do not associate anyone with Him.

In order to console the Prophet ﷺ from the after-effects of Uhud, he is addressed in a unique manner: "*[O Prophet] it was thanks to Allah's Mercy that you were gentle to them. Had you been rough or hard-hearted, they would surely have scattered away from you. So, pardon them, pray for their forgiveness, and take counsel from them in matters [of importance]. And when you are resolved on a course of action, put your trust in Allah. Surely, Allah loves those who put their trust in Him. If Allah helps you, none shall prevail over you, but if He forsakes you, then who can help you? So, in Allah let the believers put their trust.*" (Al 'Imran 3: 159–160)

Universal Principles of Good Governance and Organizational Excellence

Two extremely important aspects of good governance are touched upon by the Qur'an in the above *ayat*. First, the Prophet ﷺ has a kind nature and his heart was filled with *rahmah*, "*We have sent you forth as nothing but mercy to people of the world.*" (*al-Anbiya'* 21: 107) The Prophet's kind and loving attitude towards his followers conquered their hearts and minds. His love and compassion prevailed over any sort of authoritarian conduct. In other words, Islamic leadership must be compassionate and loving; not proud, harsh or authoritarian in nature. Second, the Prophet ﷺ is advised to observe *shura*, i.e., consultation and counselling in all strategic matters. If we look critically at the Prophet's practice, we will realize that the decisions to go out and fight at Badr as well as Uhud were made after extensive *shura*. In both cases, the Prophet ﷺ preferred the views of the *Sahabah* over his own opinion. The institution of *shura*, consequently, becomes a major characteristic of an ideal Islamic political system and mode of governance for all times and places.

The ethics of *shura* is to deliberate a matter from different viewpoints; but when a consensus is arrived at, it must be followed with complete trust in Allah, and must be owned by everyone involved in the consultation. *Shura*, therefore, means expounding various options and solutions, then selecting out of them the most appropriate proposition according to the principles of *Shari'ah*, and finally, leaving the consequences to Allah with full trust in Him. The ethics of *shura* make the leader, the Amir, the CEO, obliged to follow the consensus view (*'azun al-umur*) of the participants. He cannot veto the *shura*, because Allah's *barakah* or blessing is with the *jama'ah*. This kills the dictatorial psyche of the leadership, and it educates all stakeholders on how to sacrifice their own view and accept others' opinions.

The principle followed in *shurawi* decision-making is not always prevailing of majority over a minority view. Even a minority view if based on an evident command (*hukm*) or directive of Allah or the Prophet ﷺ, prevails over personal views of a majority, decisions, therefore are principled and not personal.

Shura also develops ownership in the group, whereby no one is allowed to advocate his/her personal position against the collective opinion after a decision has been made. This closes the doors to division within the *ummah* and, at a micro level, within any organization. Organizational excellence can be achieved only when those in authority and others within the organization are on one and the same page; and have a firm commitment to the vision and mission of the organization.

The Negative Role of the *Munafiqun*

The *munafiqun* of Madinah were always looking for issues on which they could create a division and conflict among the believers. One misgiving they created was that if the Prophet ﷺ was a genuine Messenger of Allah, then the Muslims should have defeated the Makkans in Uhud. They also opposed the Prophet's strategy of going out of Madinah to fight, as according to them, that showed a lack of concern for his own people's lives. The Qur'an refers to the baselessness of their criticism, while maintaining that a Prophet can never be dishonest towards his people: "*It is not [appropriate] for a Prophet to defraud; and whoever defrauds shall bring with him the fruit of his fraud on the Day of Resurrection. Then every soul shall be paid in full what it has earned, and none will be wronged. Is he who follows the good pleasure of Allah like him who is laden with Allah's wrath and whose abode is Hell?*" (Al 'Imran 3: 161–162) In continuation, the Qur'an further elaborates that the Prophet ﷺ is constantly guided by his *Rabb*. Therefore, it is not possible for him to go astray. But the *munafiqun* who are guided by their malice, anger and indignation towards the believers may temporarily enjoy their worldly pleasures, although their ultimate abode is the Hellfire. When raising their objections, the *munfiqun* totally ignore the conquest of Badr and the policy of the Prophet ﷺ to make decisions with consultation or *shura* as directed by the Qur'an.

The unsurpassable justice (*'adl*) of Allah is reflected in the following *ayah* which refers to grading even among the hypocrites. Allah knows well how deep each one of them is in their dislike of Islam and this will be judged according to their level of *nifaq*: "*They vary greatly in rank in the sight of Allah, and Allah sees what they do.*" (Al 'Imran 3: 163)

The *munafiqun* never welcomed the coming of *wahi*, revelation, because it disclosed their conspiracies and plans to harm the believers. They also disliked the Prophet ﷺ despite his soft-heartedness and forgiving nature. The Qur'an underscores the appointment of the Prophet ﷺ as humanity's guide, role model, and as a blessing for the believers due to his soft-heartedness, kind behaviour, and love and concern for the success of the believers in the life Hereafter: "*Allah conferred a great favour on the believers when He raised from among them a Messenger to recite to them His ayat, to purify them, and to teach them the Book and Wisdom. For before that they were in manifest error.*" (Al 'Imran 3: 164)

The Dynamic Role of the Prophet ﷺ

The discourse on the reformatory role of the Prophets' leadership is a major theme in the Qur'an. Prophet Musa played a leadership role in the liberation of the Bani Isra'il from the oppressive rule of the Pharaoh. But that is only one dimension of a reformatory leader. The Qur'an elaborates on the comprehensive leadership of the Prophets of Allah at four interlinked levels.

First and foremost, as the custodians of revelation, they get direct *hidayah* from Allah. They deliver the message as it is, without a single addition or deletion of a dot or a comma. In the case of the Final Messenger ﷺ, even before he was commissioned as Messenger ﷺ, the people of Makkah called him the most truthful (*al-Sadiq*) and the trustworthy (*al-Amin*). This is why they never questioned the Prophet's honesty and truthfulness; rather, they questioned the revelation (*wahi*) and its Divinity—even though they could not produce a single verse (*ayah*) like that of the Qur'an. This was because, while they did use the same words and alphabet of the Arabic language, the construction of the Qur'anic statements was Divine and not capable of being produced by a human. Therefore, the Prophet ﷺ, and his followers after him, have a responsibility to communicate the Message of the Qur'an as it is, to the whole of mankind and let the people decide about accepting it or rejecting it.

The Prophet ﷺ also made sure that the revelation was judicially preserved in its original form. Instant memorization and committing it to writing was done by persons designated as scribes. The Prophet ﷺ himself would recite the verses of revelation in his five daily prayers, and he used to educate a good number of *Sahabah* at the *suffah*, an academy established within the mosque of the Prophet ﷺ.

The second responsibility of the Prophets of Allah, as specified by the Qur'an, is to teach and educate, to do *tashrih* of the Book (*ta'lim* and *sharah* of the Book). In this aspect, Prophet Muhammad ﷺ elaborated and explained the Book—first, by his own conduct and behaviour, as mentioned by the Mother of the Believers, 'A'ishah who said that 'his *khuluq* was the Qur'an'; and second, by his verbal elaboration whenever a question was raised or whenever he felt the need to illustrate an *ayah* of the Qur'an. In other words, he was essentially an educator (*mu'allim*) and a role model. He consistently demonstrated how Allah's commands were to be implemented, such that his model of conduct (*uswah*) became an illustration of the entire *Shari'ah* and *ahkam* of Allah. Additionally, whatever he did, said or endorsed, as the Final Messenger ﷺ, was declared to be part of the *Shari'ah* by the Lawgiver Allah: "*He who obeys the Messenger, obeys Allah...*" (al-Nisa' 4: 80) In other words, the Messenger is both *sharih* and *shari'*, i.e., he interprets and translates the *Shari'ah*, and also legislates the *Shari'ah*, himself.

Third, the Prophets of Allah impart wisdom (*hikmah*), which is more than just conveying information, knowledge, or education. *Hikmah* stands for the purpose, objective, and benefit behind any act. It is a special gift from Allah given to the Prophets and a selected number of Allah-conscious persons, like Khizr in the story of Musa. A consensus exists on the view that Prophet Muhammad's *hikmah* is preserved in the shape of Hadith and Sunnah, which provide details about his conduct, decisions, and behaviour. It is in this sense that the Qur'an declares: "*Surely, there was a good example for you in the Messenger of Allah—for all those who look forward to Allah and the Last Day, and remember Allah much.*" (al-Ahzab 33: 21) "Good example" simply means a role model which is realistic, universal, and complete.

The fourth responsibility of the Prophets pertains to their reformatory role, which—first and foremost, by their own conduct—provides an example of how to be pious, virtuous, Allah-conscious, and soft-hearted through the purification of the soul and mind. All these aspects, with respect to the Final Prophet ﷺ, are fully preserved in the Hadith and *sirah* literature, and in the continuous practice of his Sunnah by the believers. There is no room or need for someone else to invent ways of doing purification (*tazkiyah*) of the self (*nafs*), soul (*ruh*) or heart (*qalb*) in the presence of the best model of *tazkiyah* provided by the Prophetic *uswah* and Sunnah. There is no authentic way (*tariqah*) except the Sunnah of the Final Messenger ﷺ.

After setting the record straight, that the Prophet ﷺ is a blessing for the whole of mankind, the Qur'an addresses the *munafiqun* of Madinah about their irrationality in blaming the Prophet ﷺ for the consequences of Uhud: "*And how come when a calamity befell you, even though the enemy had suffered at your hands [in the Battle of Badr] twice what you have suffered, you began to ask, 'How has this come about?' Say [O Prophet]: 'This calamity has been brought about by yourselves. Surely, Allah has power over everything.' What befell you on the day when the two hosts met was by the leave of Allah and in order that He might mark out those who believe from those who are hypocrites. And when it was said to them [the hypocrites]: 'Come and fight in the way of Allah or [at least] defend yourselves,' they answered: 'If we but knew that there would be fighting, we would certainly have followed you.' They were on that day nearer to infidelity than faith. They utter from their mouths what is not in their hearts. Allah knows well what they conceal. [These are] the ones who stayed away saying about their brothers, 'Had they followed us, they would not have been slain.' Say [O Prophet]: 'Avert death from yourselves, if you speak the truth.'*" (Al 'Imran 3: 165–168)

Elevation of the Martyrs (*Shuhada'*)

Two types of personalities emerged out of the test and trial of Badr and Uhud. One type comprised of those who aspired for a comfortable life in this world and did not want to take any risk by participating in *jihad*. This included the hypocrites who, under the pretext that their view was not accepted by the Prophet ﷺ, withdrew from war against the *mushrikin* in Badr and Uhud; whereas they were truly only afraid of death. The other type of personality was of those who believed consciously in *tawhid*, that Allah is All-Powerful, that He is the only Protector and Supporter of the believers, and that every single soul must pass away at an already fixed time; therefore, participating in a war against the *mushrikin* did not scare them.

These believers knew that those who offer their lives and resources in the cause of Islam and in obedience to Allah and His Messenger ﷺ are elevated to the highest possible stations in the life Hereafter. The Qur'an declares that they shall be welcomed in Paradise and will have the company of the Prophets, the honest and truthful persons (*siddiqin*), and of those known as *sulaha'* for their piety. The Qur'an describes such martyrs (*shuhada'*) as living, and not dead, and how they are sustained and are fed is known only to Allah.

The *munafiqun*, on the other hand, lament when they think of those who went to fight and sacrificed their lives. They think that had they not gone to war, they could have averted their death. The Qur'an refers to the true believers, who gave their lives in the way of Allah, as persons who are welcomed in *Jannah* and they rejoice while experiencing the favours given to them in the Paradise: "*Think not of those slain in the way of Allah as dead. Indeed, they are alive with their Lord, well-provided for, rejoicing in what Allah has bestowed upon them out of His bounty, and jubilant for those yet to join them but are left behind (in this world); that there will be no fear for them nor will they grieve. They rejoice at the favours and bounties of Allah and (at the awareness) that Allah will not cause the reward of the believers to be lost. There were those who responded to the call of Allah and the Messenger after injury had smitten them. Those of them who do good and fear Allah will have a mighty reward.*" (Al 'Imran 3: 169–172)

"*When people said to them: 'Indeed a host has gathered against you and you should fear them,' it only increased their faith and they answered: 'Allah is sufficient for us and what an excellent Guardian He is!' So, they returned with the favour and bounty from Allah, having suffered no harm. They followed the good pleasure of Allah, and Allah is [the] Lord of great bounty. It was Satan who wronged you to have fear of his allies. But do not fear them, fear Me, if you truly believe.*" (Al 'Imran 3: 173–175)

The Attitude of *Munafiqun*

The Qur'an mentions that the *munafiqun* are attracted to worldly gains, which are short-lived when compared to the gains and losses in the life Hereafter. When they enjoy worldly pleasures, they consider them to be blessings from Allah to them, while the fact of the matter is that all worldly comforts are a test to see how grateful they are to their Lord and the Provider of whatever they enjoy in this world. Their ungratefulness only wins them permanent chastisement in the life Hereafter. The Qur'an also corrects their perception by stating that perhaps their collaboration with the *mushrikin* will result in blocking the spread of Islam. Events like Uhud, on the other hand, helped the believers to discover who the black sheep were in the community; they got fully exposed and identified.

"*Let not those who run towards unbelief grieve you; they shall not hurt Allah in the least. Allah will not provide for them any share in the Hereafter. Theirs shall be a mighty chastisement. Indeed, those who have purchased unbelief in exchange for faith shall not hurt Allah in the least. Theirs shall be a painful chastisement.*" (Al 'Imran 3: 176–177)

The negative thinking of the *munafiqun* was reflected in their sarcastic remarks on the beautiful Qur'anic way of persuading the believers to perform *infaq* and spending (*sadaqat*) for the sake of Allah's pleasure. The Qur'an eloquently motivates the believers, when it asks: "*Who will lend his Lord a goodly loan...?*" (al-Hadid 57: 11) Naturally, Allah owns everything in the universe. He does not need any help from anyone; He helps everyone and is above all kinds of help. In their envy, they taunt that Allah has become (*na'udhu billah*) short of funds and is therefore seeking a loan! They cover up their niggardliness with such unbecoming gestures and statements.

The hypocrites exploit the word loan (*qard*) used in the Qur'an for persuading the believers to do *infaq* and *sadaqat* as their social obligation. They fail to understand what kind of *qard* Allah is asking for. This is a unique *qard* because it is none other than the One Who is the giver of every single thing to human beings—the One Who gives them life and resources—is asking to contribute on a unique condition that if this loan (*qard*) is given with sincerity, it shall be returned to them in the life Hereafter, multiplied by seven hundred times or more. Should not a person feel grateful for such a noble offer! Or must they taunt, be sarcastic and mock! The *munafiqun* of Madinah raised such typical questions, as their forefathers had raised earlier toward the Prophets and Messengers sent to Bani Isra'il.

The Bani Isra'il challenged the authority of their Prophets and demanded very specific miracles such as that of an offering, which is made to Allah, to be consumed by a heavenly fire. They declared that unless they see such miracles with their own eyes, they shall not consider the Prophet ﷺ as truthful. They are then reminded of their own history that even when offerings on their behalf were made by their Prophets and were consumed by a Divine fire, they still disobeyed and killed their Prophets. They are warned about a severe punishment awaiting them in the life Hereafter. However, those who consider this worldly life as an interval and do good deeds in this short period are promised permanent bliss and joy in the life Hereafter.

At this point, the Qur'an once again reminds the unbelievers and the hypocrites that though they act in a rebellious manner, Allah, out of His Magnanimity, does not withdraw His countless favours that He has made to them. This is to let them realize how ungrateful and unfair they are. With the Wisdom best known to Him, He grants them extra time and opportunities to return to Him. But when the time limit expires, no one can save them from His anger in this world and in the Hereafter.

"Let not the unbelievers imagine that the respite We grant them is good for them. We grant them respite so they may grow in wickedness. Theirs will be a humiliating chastisement.

Allah will not let the believers stay in the state they are: He will set the wicked apart from the good. Allah is not going to disclose to you what is hidden in the unseen [realm], but He chooses from among His Messengers whom He wills (to intimate such knowledge). So, believe in Allah and in His Messenger. And if you believe and become Allah conscious, yours will be a great reward.

Let not those who are niggardly about what Allah granted them out of His bounty think that niggardliness is good for them; rather it is bad for them. What they were niggardly about will turn into a halter around their necks on the Day of Resurrection. To Allah belongs the inheritance of the heavens and the earth. Allah is All-Aware of what you do.

Indeed, Allah has heard the saying of those who said: 'Allah is poor, and we are rich.' We shall record what they have said, and [the fact of] their slaying the Prophets unjustly. And We shall say [to them]: 'Taste the torment of burning. That is [in recompense] for what your hands have sent forth [i.e., your own deed]). Allah does no injustice to His servants.'

[They are] those who say: 'Allah has directed us that we accept none as Messenger until he makes an offering that the fire will consume.' Say [O Prophet]): 'Other Messengers did in fact come to you before me with Clear Signs and with the sign you have mentioned. So why did you slay them, if what you say is true?'

[Now] if they denied you, so too were Messengers before you who came with Clear Signs, Scriptures and the illuminating Book. Every soul is bound to taste death, and you shall receive your full reward on the Day of Resurrection. Then whoever is spared the Fire and is admitted to Paradise has indeed been successful. The life of this world is merely an illusory enjoyment." (Al 'Imran 3: 178–185)

POINT TO PONDER

The charms of glamorous and joyful living should not make us unmindful of our obligations towards our *Rabb* and His creations. He is the real Owner of whatever He has bestowed to us. He has provided them to us as an *amanah* or trust. It is our obligation as the trustees to feed the hungry, help the needy, give to the deserving, and thank Allah for giving us plentiful opportunities to do good.

A *munafiq* yearns for worldly pleasures and comforts, while a believer yearns for Allah's pleasure (*rida*) even when they may have to suffer in this worldly life. A believer learns to feel content and pleased in difficulties because Allah provides ease for the believer along with and after every difficulty. Allah is the Most Generous, Most Caring, Most Loving.

Worldly attractions and charms are one of the most effective tools of Satan. It is not only the *mushrikun* and *munafiqun* who are influenced by worldly cravings and gains; the *mu'minun* can be equally influenced. It is a test for the believers as well as the non-believers. In other words, even believers must be constantly wary of satanic traps and charms. One should be aware that while it is a blessing of Allah to enjoy a wholesome family life, there is also a test, *fitnah* in one's wealth and children. Believers must seek Allah's help (*isti'anah*) and protection (*isti'adhah*) from the whispers of Satan by seeking forgiveness (*istighfar*) from Allah and by engaging in His remembrance (*dhikr*) through *salah*, *sadaqat*, *sabr* and *istiqamah*. These things alone can protect a believer from the charms of Satan.

"*You [believers] will certainly be put to test in regard to your wealth and lives, and you will certainly hear many hurtful things from those who were granted the Book before you and [from] the polytheists. But if you remain patient and mindful of Allah, this indeed is a matter of great resolution.*" (Al 'Imran 3: 186)

The Essential Unity in the Message

The fact of matter, known to the people of the Book, was that their scholars (*ulema*) and saints (*masha'ikh*) used to twist, modify and even change the words in their Scriptures according to their own interests. Consequently, inner conflicts and disagreement appeared in the Books, which their scribes wrote and modified; they also hid portions of the Book.

The Qur'an insists that their own Books were revealed to their Prophets by One and the same source, Allah, the Lord of the Universe. All Prophets had one common message, i.e., uncompromising obedience to the Creator and the Owner of the Day of Judgement. But the People of the Book twisted, changed, and tried to cover up the Truth in exchange for short-lived worldly gains: "*[Recall] when Allah took a covenant from those who were given the Book: 'You shall explain it to people and not hide it.' Then they cast it behind their backs and sold it away for trivial gain. Evil indeed is their bargain!*

Do not let those who rejoice in their misdeeds and love to be praised for what they have not done, think that they are secure from chastisement. Theirs will be a painful chastisement. To Allah belongs the dominion of the heavens and earth. And Allah is All-Powerful." (Al 'Imran 3: 187–189) The Qur'an invites them to follow the Truth contained in it, as the Final Revelation to the whole of mankind, which confirms basic teachings conveyed by the earlier Prophets of Allah.

While approaching the end of the *surah,* believers are gifted with a beautiful supplication which summarizes the purpose and objectives of human life and revalidates the faith of the believers. In the earlier *ayat*, non-believers were told about the chastisement awaiting the evil-doers in the life Hereafter. Now believers are guided in how to approach their *Rabb* for forgiveness and seek the best reward in the *Akhirah.*

The Supplication

First, a believer is advised to use his/her faculties of observation, hearing and introspection, and to look curiously and critically into the great blessings and favours Allah has made on them; how the Creator, the Best of all Planners has created the heavens and earth; how He has set up the alternation of night and day; how a biological cycle is created in all animate beings, whether humans, animals, birds or fish; how the sleep cycle provides physical and psychological relief and comfort to human beings; and how, if this cycle is disturbed, then the human mind and body are stressed and face drastic effects on their performance. Prayer, *salah,* is a blessing from Allah in that it provides us an opportunity to humble ourselves and show gratefulness to the Creator (*Khaliq*) Allah for His countless favours upon us. Therefore, it is mentioned that the people of understanding remember Allah with thankfulness—while standing in *salah,* when they bend down, and prostrate, also while sitting in prayer, and even when they rest by reclining on their sides. They remember Him with His beautiful names and by reciting portions of the Qur'an from memory.

Unlike many world religions, the Qur'an, on practically every page invites its readers to ponder, reflect, examine, investigate and study nature, the world and the universe around us, as well as one's own biological constitution and the synergy within the human body, brain and mind, and soul. The more a person explores, the more one gets convinced about the existence, of the One and Only Living Creator and Sustainer Allah: "*Surely, in the creation of the heavens and earth and in the alternation of night and day, there are Signs for people of understanding. [They are] those who remember Allah while standing, sitting or [reclining] on their backs, and reflect in the creation of the heavens and earth, [saying]: 'Our Lord! You have not created this in vain. Glory to You! Save us from the chastisement of the Fire. Our Lord! Whomsoever You cause to enter the Fire, him You indeed bring to disgrace, and there will be none to succor the wrongdoers.'"* (Al 'Imran 3: 190–192)

With this statement of facts, a believer surrenders his/her whole being to the Lord of the heavens and the earth, while thanking Him for not leaving mankind without showing them the Right Path to success and forgiveness: "*Our Lord! We indeed, heard a caller calling to the faith saying: 'Believe in your Lord,' so we believed. Our Lord! Forgive us our sins, wipe out our evil deeds, and make us die with the truly pious. Our Lord! Fulfil what You promised us through Your Messengers and disgrace us not on the Day of Resurrection—indeed, You never go back on Your promise.*" (Al 'Imran 3: 193–194)

The one who is All-Merciful, All-Forgiving, All-Compassionate and All-Hearing listens to the sincere request of His servant. Indeed, His *rahmah* transcends all possible limits: "*So their Lord answered the prayers thus: 'I will not let go to waste the work of any of you—male or female. Each of you is from the other. Those who emigrated and were driven out from their homesteads and were persecuted in My cause, and who fought and were slain, indeed I shall wipe out their evil deeds from them and shall certainly admit them to the Gardens beneath which rivers flow.' This is their reward with their Lord and with Allah lies the best reward.*" (Al 'Imran 3: 195)

These *ayat* make crystal clear the high status of the believers who emigrate in the cause of Islam and who are persecuted in their own homelands because of their steadfastness (*istiqamah*) on Islam. Similarly, those who sacrifice their lives in the way of Allah are promised a great reward in the life Hereafter.

Humbling oneself in front of Allah, with full trust and dependence on Him, is an indication of servitude. On the contrary, walking with pride and striking the floor with arrogance indicates vanity and pomposity in a person. For those who walk a walk of pride, utter humiliation awaits them in the life Hereafter: "*[O Prophet] do not let the pompous walk of the unbelievers in the land deceive you. It is but a trifling and fleeting enjoyment, then their destination is Hell—what an evil place to rest!*" (Al 'Imran 3: 196–197)

On the other hand, the Most Forgiving and Most Compassionate says the following about those who sincerely submit to their Lord and live a life of Allah-consciousness (*taqwa*): "*But those who fear their Lord, theirs shall be Gardens beneath which rivers flow, and therein they will live forever—a hospitality from Allah. And what is with Allah is best for the pious. Indeed, among the People of the Book, some believe in Allah and what has been revealed to you and what has been revealed to them. They humble themselves before Allah, and do not sell Allah's revelation for a trivial gain. For such, their reward lies with their Lord. Allah is swift in reckoning.*" (Al 'Imran 3: 198–199)

Approaching the end of the *surah*, believers are reminded of their real resources: steadfastness (*istiqamah*) and connecting themselves to Allah (*i'tisam billah*), which help in overcoming all problems, hardships and hinderances. Believers are told to develop consistency (*istiqamah*), persistence (*sabr*) and regularity in their servitude to their *Rabb*. In other words, obedience to Allah is not subject to any specific day or time. It is a matter of total life commitment. Therefore, persistence and perseverance are not only to be observed by one's own self, but also to be shared and communicated to others through continuous practice of *ma'ruf, 'amal al-salih,* and *taqwa*. This brings the hearts of the believers together. They advise (*nasihah*) each other to excel in the love and obedience of Allah and His Messenger ﷺ, which in turn increases their Allah-consciousness (*taqwa*), needed for success in this world and in the Hereafter: "*O Believers! Be steadfast, vie in steadfastness, stand firm [in your faith], and be mindful of Allah, so that you may be successful.*" (Al 'Imran 3: 200)

Take Home Points

At the end of this *surah*, we are reminded of the importance and centrality of certain behavioural characteristics which are a pre-requisite for success in this world and in the Hereafter. First and foremost is Allah-consciousness (*taqwa*). We know that *Surah al-Baqarah* begins with the theme of *taqwa* and elaborates further who the *muttaqun* are. *Surah Al 'Imran*, which has a thematic continuity with *al-Baqarah*, also underscores this behavioural category, without which no achievement can be made. Spending generously in the way of Allah (*infaq, sadaqat*) is another important value, underscored in the beginning of both *al-Baqarah* and *Al 'Imran*. Similarly, reliance on the help and support of Allah (*tawakkul*) and the steadfastness and persistence (*istiqamah*) in the struggle (*jihad*) for the establishment of the *din*, truth, justice, security and peace, are the contributing factors toward success, highlighted in both *surahs*.

Establishment of the *din*, as discussed earlier, is a much wider theme. Its first laboratory is one's own self (*nafs*). Allah's *hakimiyyah*, Sovereignty, should be fully realized in, at least, a person's own life, in their home, their profession and in their social behaviour. The second domain is a person's family. Not only the husband, wife and children, but parents and all blood and legal relations (including the in-laws) should also be approached with *hikmah* to join in the *iqamah* of the *din*—through healthy social interactions, by observing Allah's commands and avoiding the *munkarat*.

One's profession is another domain of *iqamah*. How far a professional observes Islamic ethics and manners in his/her social transactions, in his/her speech, in avoiding gender-mixing and in observing honesty, *amanah* and fairness (*'adl*), determine how well they strive to establish the *din*. One must ensure that a person's earning and spending is *halal* and *haram*-free. In brief, *iqamah* of the *din* includes a wider range of human activities. It encompasses social, economic, and political behaviour as integral to each other.

The total change and transformation that Islam visualizes can take place only when the key prerequisites of *iman*, *taqwa*, *sabr*, *salah*, *infaq*, *jihad fi sabilillah* and dissemination of Islamic truth (*da'wah*) are manifested in personal, social, economic, political and cultural dealings. If one is lacking in any of these key factors, they end up in a gray area and may not qualify for success. It is another thing that Allah, out of His enormous *rahmah,* Mercy and Compassion, may disregard our shortcomings; but as true *muttaqun*, we must strive to give our best, seeking the pleasure of Allah and fearing His punishment.

The *surah* ends on an important *nasihah*, a vital directive: "*O Believers! Be steadfast [isbiru], vie in steadfastness [sabiru], stand firm [in your faith] [rabitu], and be mindful of Allah [ittaqu], so that you may be successful.*" (Al 'Imran 3: 200)

This last *ayah* advises us on three vital behavioural traits. First, to have an unwavering, firm and unshakable attitude against the forces of evil, *kufr* and *taghut*. At the same time, to advise believers to be steadfast in guarding and protecting the Muslim identity, Muslim territories and interests, while fully observing the *salah* at its appointed times. This theme is further elaborated by the Qur'an in *Surah al-'Asr*, where it educates the believers that only those believers who have firm faith, act ethically and advise each other to hold fast to truth and to be steadfast, are the ones to have avoided ending up in a loss.

The experiences of Badr and Uhud reconfirm that Muslims can only succeed when they make sincere efforts in the cause of Allah, obey the Prophet's directions, and observe *sabr,* steadfastness *(istiqamah)* and seek Allah's Help, *isti'anah* and observe truthfulness.

This *surah* also ends on a directive to not only be firm and steadfast in the realization of the *din* but also to advise (do *da'wah*), educate and convince members of the community to perseverance, *istiqamah*, solidarity, Allah-consciousness, giving *nasihah* to one's own self, near relatives and members of society and continuing to seek Allah's forgiveness at all times.

Wa ma tawfiqi illa billah